To my sister –

You're always in my heart

Merry Christmas with love

Tom
12/02

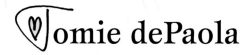

# Tomie dePaola

## HIS ART & HIS STORIES

# Tomie dePaola

## HIS ART & HIS STORIES

by Barbara Elleman

G. P. PUTNAM'S SONS  NEW YORK

♥ *To Don,*
*my anchor and my beacon*

———————————————

G. P. Putnam's Sons,
a division of Penguin Putnam Books for Young Readers,
345 Hudson Street, New York, NY 10014. G. P. Putnam's Sons,
Reg. U.S. Pat. & Tm. Off. Published simultaneously in Canada.
Printed in Hong Kong by South China Printing Co. (1988) Ltd.
Book design by Donna Mark. Text set in Garth Graphic.
Library of Congress Cataloging-in-Publication Data
Elleman, Barbara. Tomie dePaola, his art and his stories /
Barbara Elleman.  p.  cm. Includes bibliographical references.
1. dePaola, Tomie. 2. Authors, American—20th century—Biography.
3. Illustrators—United States—Biography. 4. Children's stories—
Authorship. 5. Illustration of books. I. Title.  PS3554.E117Z65   1999
813'.54—dc21 [B] 98-19821  CIP   ISBN 0-399-23129-3
10  9  8  7  6  5  4  3  2

# Contents

# Preface

---

Once upon a time in the 1970s, for some now forgotten reason, I decided to do an illustration in the style of Tomie dePaola. A clever forgery was actually what I was after, and I clearly remember thinking that it would take ten or twenty minutes of my time, tops. I'd always had a knack for imitating different drawing and handwriting styles, and I was sure I could knock off a "Tomie" drawing as easy as pie for the book jacket or a birthday card or whatever it was I was doing.

I sat down at my drawing table with the three-hundred-pound Fabriano watercolor paper, the stacks of colored pencils, the best watercolors, and all the art supplies that I knew Tomie was fond of using. Six hours later, sweaty, frustrated, and thoroughly puzzled, I tore up the thirty-eighth ruined piece of paper in despair. No matter how hard I tried—in fact, the harder I tried—the further I got from success; I could not imitate Tomie's way of drawing. That seemingly formulaic style, with its simple line, its folksy composition, and its childlike color, was a lot more complex and sophisticated than I had bargained for—and almost impossible to duplicate in spirit.

Like almost everyone else, I was looking at the surface of things and making the wrong assumptions. I'd forgotten about the old standard myth that also happens to be true: the artist always draws or paints him- or herself, no matter what the subject and no matter what or how the approach. We illustrators create and re-create ourselves over and over—not just in the ways our unwitting pens and brushes draw sets of features that look much more like ourselves than, say, the enchanted frog, but in the very atmosphere, tone, and approach we lay down for a story. You can tell a whole lot about an illustrator's spirit and personal stuff from his or her illustrations.

Tomie's illustrations are just like Tomie: They look easy but they're not. He's a puzzle and an enigma. He's also a lot of fun and hard to ignore. I've been Tomie's friend for almost twenty-five years, and I am still not sure who he is. I have come to think of him as a force of nature: comforting, playful, and nurturing sometimes; stormy, scornful, and angry at others. And sometimes he's just not there! He travels around the whole world like Old Mother West Wind or the North Wind in Norse fairy tales—here today, gone tomorrow. I call Tomie to ask a question and get his assistant, Bob. "So, hey, Bob, how ya doing? Where's Tomie?" Bob says, "In Australia." Wow! Here one day, gone the next!

Nevertheless, when Tomie and I get together, it's usually a happy place to be. Tomie can laugh and be silly and carry on like nobody else in this world. Tomie's house and gardens are always beautiful, stunning, and the most fantastic place you can visit in this part of the New England landscape.

I always think that Tomie's house should be transplanted to New Mexico. I can't understand why he lives in New Hampshire, except that that's just the other part of Tomie—he won't ever give up. He's strong, stubborn, witty, and tough. He's Irish! He's Italian! He's gone before you know it, and there when you think he's gone. He's our hero; a Connecticut Yankee disguised as Mother Goose. Everybody loves Tomie because his books are basically loved, needed, and meaningful. They're a lot of fun, and hard to ignore; playful, thoughtful, enigmatic, and impossible to imitate (maybe he uses a magic crayon). He's a well-crafted legend and a searching, grown-up child. And all of that with such ease and joy and confidence. *Viva Tomie!*

Trina Schart Hyman
LYME, NH
JUNE 1998

# Introduction

For Tomie dePaola, 26 Fairmount Avenue, Meriden, Connecticut, represents both an old childhood address and a new series of chapter books designed to reach children older than his picture book audience. And while the distance between that small town in southeastern Connecticut and the even smaller town of New London, New Hampshire, where the artist-author lives today, isn't far, for dePaola the journey has been a full complement of twists, turns, backtracking, and straightaways. Nevertheless, it has fulfilled a self-proclaimed childhood prophecy. "I am going to be an artist when I grow up, and write stories and draw pictures for books, and sing and tap-dance on the stage," dePaola told his family when he was just four years old. Not many people may have heard about his professional tap-dancing stint, which did happen in the now-closed Madeira Club in Provincetown, Massachusetts, in 1964, but his impact on the world of children's books is secure and far-reaching. At this writing, more than five million copies of his books are in print in fifteen countries.

Having begun his career in 1965, dePaola will celebrate his thirty-fifth year in publishing in the year 2000 with a total of 205 books illustrated, about a hundred of which he also wrote. While his prolific output has been the source of comment and criticism over the years, dePaola's response is philosophical: "I work fast. Once, this kind of criticism bothered me, but no longer. Children never complain that I do too many books, and they are my true audience."

His abilities to know what appeals to children and to translate those interests and desires to image and text are at the core of dePaola's success. It is what makes his work so lasting and what has continued to reach children for more than thirty years. As writer Nancy Cobb remarked so succinctly in *The Hartford Courant,* dePaola has "a tender and innate understanding of what children need."[1] Fads and trends come and go, and while a number of dePaola's books have faded into oblivion (some justifiably so), titles such as *Nana Upstairs & Nana Downstairs,* *"Charlie Needs a Cloak,"* *Strega Nona,* *The Clown of God,* and *The Art Lesson,* which charmed their way into children's hearts at the time of publication and continue to be favorites generations later, will undoubtedly claim an audience far into the twenty-first century.

In this retrospective study, I've tried to give a hint of the man behind the art and his stories while concentrating on places where his personal and professional lives overlap, identifying patterns and motifs that make his work unique, showing the major influences on his art, and giving readers a broader appreciation of his style and techniques.

Over the past year and a half, dePaola opened his files, personal library, and original art collection to my scrutiny, and made time for formal interviews and wide-ranging casual conversations. His generosity allowed greater insights into his work than otherwise would have been possible. While the quotes and sources are given credit in the appendix, the observations and comments are mine. I began following Tomie dePaola's work early in his career—around the same time I began my years as a reviewer at *Booklist.* I continued to be intrigued through my years as Children's Editor at *Booklist* and then as Editor in Chief of *Book Links;* his technique, style, and themes have interested me for more than twenty-five years. Revisiting his books has been a joyful and rewarding visual experience; I hope I have done his work justice.

*Barbara Elleman*

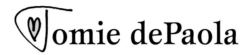

# Tomie dePaola

## HIS ART & HIS STORIES

"I use my garden like I use my paints."

# A Life

------------

Stepping into Tomie dePaola's home is much like walking into the pages of the artist-author's books. While one is subliminally aware of the thoughtfully controlled design, the eye focuses on the feast of color (flowers, fruit, and greenery), the array of art objects both solemn (a folk-art sculpture of the Lady of Guadalupe) and amusing (three life-size fleece-covered Rocky Mountain goats standing in the entryway), and the surprising details (carved wooden blackbirds caught in flight) that promise a story. But what permeates both house and book is the abiding warmth and conviviality.

Without a doubt, dePaola's New London, New Hampshire, home is an artistic experience, but the human factor—his large, welcoming smile, the rush of his laugh, his exuberant greeting—is what is most memorable. His enthusiasm carries across the threshold and provides an easy cushion for free-flowing, pithy conversations about art, illustration, books, writing, folklore, research, travel, family, and life in general. In the background, Gregorian chants (from an ever-playing compact disc) filter through the rooms, while outside, his wooden deck, green-stretching lawn, and lavish flower beds meld into the aesthetic ambience. And even when dePaola is away on one of his frequent author tours, speaking engagements, or vacation jaunts, the place echoes with his effervescent personality. Yet one can sense that beneath dePaola's ebullience lies a highly complicated man with a private place that he

DePaola paintings provide
centerpieces for comfortable,
folk-art-filled rooms.

reserves for himself; and with that comes the realization that his home
is not a showcase for admirers but integral to his own artistic expression.

The large, airy rooms, which provide an apt setting for dePaola's di-
verse array of folklore objects, inevitably lead to the kitchen, where a
crowd of cookbooks, copper pots and pans, and gleaming bowls answers
his gourmet inclinations. Seven ovens—from high-tech microwave to
beehive brick—attest to his cooking skills: To dine in dePaola's home is
a culinary experience not to be forgotten.

Across a brick and plant-filled patio, a two-building barnlike structure houses his studio and Whitebird, Incorporated, the business side
of dePaola's enterprises. Here the precise layout found in the house
gives way to working clutter. Telephones ring, faxes chug out continuous messages and requests, and computers hum under the direction of
Whitebird assistant Bob Hechtel. And while sister Maureen Modine
attends to the bookkeeping, the clerical helpers, UPS drivers, and gar-
deners go about their tasks amid the friendly barking of Madison,
Markus, Morgan, and Moffat—dePaola's four Welsh terriers—and
Hechtel's large Airedale named Bingley Too (possibly the only canine
who can claim a Website named for him!).[1]

An immense collection of videos shares space with pieces of dePaola's
framed art, while boxes of letters from children, packets of publicity

DePaola gathers his terriers
for a moment of quiet.

brochures, and cartons of new books vie for space on floor and tables. Here and there a stuffed Mother Goose, a Big Anthony puppet, and a cardboard Bill and Pete (commercial and child-made versions sent by admirers) reflect the broader aspects of today's children's book business.

Above in the loft, glass doors protect copies of dePaola's 200-plus titles (including numerous foreign editions), steel cases categorize hundreds of pieces of original illustrations, and bins hold large and small paintings. Asked whether or not the latter were "fine-art" pieces destined for museum exhibitions, dePaola replied, "I call these my 'non-book' art, so as not to belittle the illustrations I do for books."

On the first floor, a connecting door leads to dePaola's private studio, built in 1997. While stacks of books in the house reflect his multisided reading tastes (everything from fiction and biography to filmography), here the walls are lined with reference books on art, illustration, folklore, and other titles necessary for his work. In the center of the room is a large drawing board surrounded by tubes of paint, colored pencils, brushes wide and narrow (dePaola calls them his household gods), bottles of water, and bits of paper cluttered with the illustrator's visual thoughts. Although he no longer uses the high stool (still claiming its original paint) from his art school days, it stands nearby. Along the walls are childhood photos and early drawings, a daily reminder of the boy dePaola once was—and still is today.

At Christmastime, candlelit windows provide a festive touch in dePaola's studio.

The Italian grandparents:
Concetta (Nana Fall-River) and
Antonio dePaola (before 1919).

The Irish grandparents:
Tom and Mary Alice (Nana
Downstairs) Downey (1955).

DePaola's parents:
Florence (Flossie) and
Joe dePaola (1928).

For what gives dePaola so much credibility with children has roots in his own life, beginning with his childhood. Born on September 15, 1934, in Meriden, Connecticut, dePaola was named Thomas Anthony after his two grandfathers—Tom Downey, his Irish grandfather, who owned a combination grocery and butcher store, and Antonio dePaola, his Italian grandfather, who died many years before dePaola was born.

His paternal grandparents, Concetta and Antonio, came from Calabria, a region in southern Italy, which the artist turned into the setting of *Strega Nona,* while his mother's ancestors emigrated from Ireland and England. Charles Parkin Mock, after arriving in the United States from Devonshire, found a job as farm foreman on an estate near New Haven, Connecticut, where he soon met and married the cook, Honorah O'Rourke, recently arrived from County Cork, Ireland. One of their three children, Mary Alice, married Thomas Lawrence Downey, also of Irish ancestry; their only daughter, Florence, known to the family as Flossie, met a man named Joseph dePaola at a dance. Their marriage in 1929 produced four children.

This large, intimate, fun-loving Irish-Italian mix, dePaola proclaims, "loved telling old tales on each other; laughter and storytelling was an everyday ingredient. My parents had such a joy of life." DePaola draws on this family joie de vivre in his depictions of the up-and-down relationships of his grandparents, aunts and uncles, siblings, and cousins—not in the tell-all, fingerpointing fashion of the 1990s, but in a warmhearted tradition of a close extended family that relishes one another's fancies and foibles.

The second child in the family, dePaola often felt overshadowed as a young boy by his older brother, Joe. Buddy, as he was called, was born four years earlier and had, according to dePaola, completely won the hearts of the entire dePaola and Downey families. "Although my mother tried to persuade everyone that I was a positive addition, the turmoil I created with my lungs didn't convince anyone."[2] Early animosities between the brothers followed through the years, and the two were never close; Joe died young, in his early forties, but dePaola's edgy relationship with his brother still strikes a raw chord.

His younger sister, Judie, who grew up mostly after dePaola left home, lives farther away, and their age difference allows fewer family memories. It is with his sister Maureen, whose birth is chronicled in *The Baby Sister,* that dePaola has always had a close association, sharing puppet making as children and partnering her in ballet performances when teenagers. While dePaola has no children of his own, his siblings

The dePaola family:
Joe Jr. (Buddy), Judie, Maureen, Tomie,
Flossie, and Joe (mid-1940's).

have ensured the continuity of the family line: DePaola has nine nieces and nephews, who in turn have produced eight children.

DePaola grew up in Depression-difficult years when money was understandably tight for a family whose only income producer was a barber. Even then, books were important. When dePaola was a toddler, his mother read to him, and his family encouraged his early artistic attempts. He recalls the excitement of getting a box of Crayola colors that contained a crayon labeled "Flesh." "With one stroke I could accomplish what none of the other forty-seven colors combined allowed me to do: fill in a human face and make it look like me."[3] And he still joyfully remembers his ninth Christmas, when all his presents were art supplies—the greatest pleasure being an easel. As his mother once said, "He took to reading at a very young age, and he always had a pencil in his hand. I remember him coming home from kindergarten one day and telling me he was going to draw pictures for books, dance and sing on stage, and paint all the scenery."[4]

A beaming two-year-old Tomie poses in the family wing chair, which, years later, becomes the prototype for the chair found in several scenes in *The Baby Sister*.

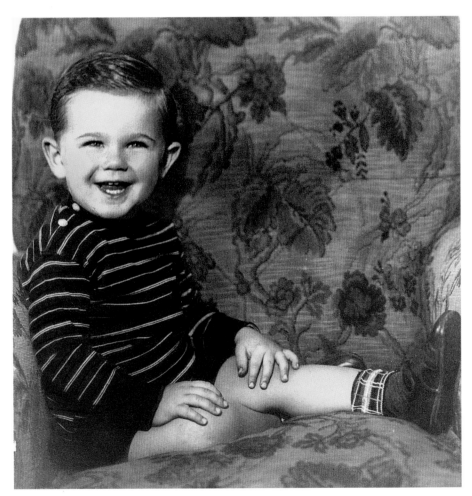

DePaola's early interest in art was, in fact, equaled by his love of the theater. When his father built him a sandbox, he turned it over and used it as a stage. Puppet shows and backyard "extravaganzas" were performed over the years, and seeing a marionette production of *King of the Golden River* is still vivid in dePaola's memory. He began tap-dancing lessons at age five, which continued until he entered art school in 1952. He paired up with friend Carol Morrissey, and the team danced their way through numerous local benefits and shows, even performing once in New York City. Years later, at dePaola's sixtieth birthday party (shared with 400 of his "closest friends"), Morrissey and dePaola re-created their "Once in Love with Amy" routine to the delight of all the partygoers. They never missed a beat!

The senior dePaola, a home-movie buff, captured many family events with his eight-millimeter camera. Relatives and neighbors from both the dePaolas' rented Oak Street and Columbus Avenue apartments in Meriden found themselves on film celebrating birthdays, relishing the Sunday funnies, eating spaghetti, decorating for Christmas, and enjoying other family happenings. One of the most significant was when the family built their own house—at 26 Fairmount Avenue. During the construction process, the budding artist found hundreds of feet of blank walls at his disposal. With a piece of blue carpenter's chalk, he created "murals" of the family on the plasterboard. Proud of his handiwork, dePaola says he was devastated when the workers covered the walls with paint. He also drew pictures on his sheets at night before going to sleep, using a penlight to guide his busy hand. Or at least he did, dePaola remembers, "until my mother stopped me."

DePaola admits to being a difficult child, partly because, he says, "I was willful and outspoken." He determinedly experimented in the kitchen. "I found out that flour and water and ketchup, deep fried, didn't taste very good, but I had to discover that for myself." In second grade, he was unable to see any reason to learn his arithmetic tables. "I, who could sing any song after hearing it once, memorize any poem, tell the plot of any movie I had seen, could not memorize my tables. As I told my teacher, I was not going to be an 'arithmetic-er'; I was going to be an artist. Furthermore, I thought it was a real waste of white paper."

Mrs. Beulah Bowers, an early art teacher who features in dePaola's book *The Art Lesson*, was more understanding of dePaola's artistic temperament; she supported his early endeavors and the two became fast friends. In fourth grade, the would-be illustrator, confident of his talent, sent a drawing to Walt Disney and was thrilled, but not surprised, to receive an answer. Mr. Disney returned the drawing, saying how im-

Tommy, the art maker, busily at work, ABOVE; BELOW, dePaola's rendering in *The Art Lesson* of his beloved art teacher, Mrs. Beulah Bowers.

13

portant it was for artists to "keep their early work" and suggesting he "continue to practice." Unfortunately, the art piece and the letter have been lost in a lifetime of moves. However, dePaola recalls, those words made such an impression on him that he takes his letters from children today seriously, realizing the impact they can have on a child.

His fifth-grade teacher, Miss Rose Mulligan, also stands out in memory. "She read aloud to us every day," dePaola remembers, "and let us dramatize a portion of Kate Douglas Wiggin's *The Birds' Christmas Carol*—one of *my* favorites—for a school Christmas assembly. She made me feel that I would, one day, be an artist."

High school, dePaola says, was "full and wonderful." And while academics were never a problem, he admits that "for a 'non-arithmetic-er' algebra was tough" and that "missing the first two weeks of my freshman year because of illness didn't help." Not surprisingly, Art Club and Props and Paints (the drama club) took much of his time, and his dancing talents earned him the title of resident choreographer for the annual variety shows and Christmas programs. And to everyone's delight, he usually turned up on the stage as well. A plum, but not unexpected, assignment came in his senior year, when he was named art editor of the school yearbook.[5]

High-stepping dePaola dances the Charleston with a friend for a Pratt Institue benefit at RIGHT; ABOVE, he partners sister Maureen for a ballet performance.

Something else he remembers from these teen years would have, unknowingly, future implications. In what became a Friday-night ritual in the dePaola home, family friends gathered regularly around the television set to watch the fights, popular fare in the 1950s. One of the visitors, Florence Nesci,[6] introduced the teenaged dePaola to the fine art of making popcorn—a treat he has been "hooked on ever since" and which was the inspiration for writing and illustrating *The Popcorn Book* some twenty years later. A large, wheeled, commercial-style popcorn maker, showing signs of much use, stands today in dePaola's barn, ready to meet current appetites.

Talking with dePaola about his childhood and teen years quickly reveals that the important events in his life and his memories of them inevitably channel—and sometimes overlap—into four areas: family, art, theater, and religion.

A case in point is his choice of art school. His mother's twin cousins, Franny and Fuffy McLaughlin, had studied at Pratt Institute in Brooklyn; by the early 1940s, they had established themselves as top-notch photographers in the magazine field.[7] DePaola also chose Pratt, a decision he attributes to the twins' influence; and the winning of a highly competitive $2000 scholarship given by the city of Meriden, made going to art school possible. Life at Pratt opened a new world for dePaola; the concentration of classes in art (except for one English class) for eight hours a day, five days a week, gave direction to his way of working for the rest of his life. "My four years at Pratt," he says, "were heaven on earth. We had working artists who gave us our specialty courses, and then a wonderful core faculty who taught us how to draw. Observe and practice, we were told, observe and practice. Keep your eyes open and draw, draw, draw."

The "us" he refers to includes now-familiar names in the children's book field: DePaola shared classes and inspiration with Anita and Arnold Lobel, Ted Lewin, Charles Mikolaycak, Cyndy Szekeres, and John Schoenherr.[8] The paths of these seven people would cross many times through the years as their expertise and reputations grew in the children's literature field. But getting there wasn't always easy. DePaola lived in a small one-room apartment on Washington Street in Brooklyn, using half the space for his studio. "I had funds one month to buy some watercolor paints and a box of corn flakes, and another month to get a piece of meat and good paper," dePaola laughingly remembers. He also recalls the need to save his money in order to buy Ruth Krauss and Maurice Sendak's then newly published *A Hole Is to Dig*, which he found "highly inventive."[9] But for his own developing tastes, the intro-

DePaola's dancing feet find their way into *Oliver Button Is a Sissy*.

Children's illustrator Anita Lobel poses with her portrait, painted by dePaola during their Pratt art school days.

duction to the folkloric style—the simple lines, carefully composed shapes, and flat perspectives—of Alice and Martin Provensen had a stronger impact.[10]

Brooklyn gave dePaola easy access to New York's many museums. It was at the Museum of Modern Art, for instance, where he indulged his love of old films, especially silent ones. Perhaps it was the combination of film and art that spurred dePaola's interest in sequence illustration[11]— a technique he effectively uses in many of his books. And, in what became a turning point in his artistic outlook, he attended a show featuring the work of the French expressionist Georges Rouault, whose desentimentalization of religious art would be a great influence.[12] "That changed my point of view. I realized that art was something more than I had thought, and I opened myself up to its influences, not so much from the aspect of illustration or commercial art but from what the fine artists were doing."

It was also during this time that he became acquainted with the work of Ben Shahn.[13] In 1955, while spending a summer studying fresco and painting at the Skowhegan School of Painting and Sculpture,[14] dePaola

DePaola presents
*Still Life with Fruit*, completed for an assignment at Pratt.

© Ray Cantu

met Shahn, who for a time became his mentor. He remembers Shahn once telling him that "Being an artist is not only what you *do* with your artwork but how you live your life" that is important.[15] In his autobiography *Between Worlds,* Leo Lionni, who also names Shahn as a mentor, says, "Shahn was fundamentally a storyteller—his paintings always refer the beholder to an event."[16] With this in mind, it is easy to see why dePaola felt a connection to Shahn's work. Although dePaola declares that it was the visions of Rouault and Shahn that were the most influential, one need only look, for instance, at Shahn's children's book *Ounce, Dice, Trice* to see a similarity of strong line and fluidity of pen stroke.[17]

DePaola's interest in fresco derived from his growing passion for contemporary liturgical art, which, in turn, had such an impact on his life and thoughts that in his junior year at Pratt he considered leaving art school to join a monastery. Dissuaded by colleagues and by Mother Placid,[18] an artist who lived in a Benedictine monastery for women in Connecticut and who became a guiding friend, he finished Pratt and, as a gift from his parents, spent a summer in Europe. "Seeing all those beautiful pieces of art that I had seen only in the pages of art-history books," dePaola remembers, "was wondrous."

The tour took an amazing turn: The ship dePaola and friends sailed on was the *Andrea Doria,* which, a week after they disembarked, was to collide with the *Stockholm* on its return journey to America and sink into the sea. Years later, the *Andrea Doria's* resting place was found and the safe retrieved from the watery depths. In a follow-up television documentary,[19] a traveler's check, written in India ink and thus clear as the day it was written, displayed the signature "Thomas dePaola."[20]

When dePaola returned from abroad, the urge to join a small monastery had not diminished, and in 1956 he made a commitment to a priory in Vermont.[21] He stayed for six months, left, returned, and left again. "I was meant to be an illustrator and writer of children's books, which was clear to me as a child, and seems clear now, but those on-and-off monastery years were an unsettling time in my life. While I still dreamed of becoming a children's book illustrator, I didn't know how to make that happen. I was living in Vermont, all the publishers were in New York, and in those days editors and art directors wanted people who were close at hand."

He hadn't stopped drawing, however. He designed Christmas cards for the Katherine Crockett Company in Vermont, produced items for a craftsmen's guild, and worked in summer theater in Weston as a set designer, even performing in several plays. And neither had he forsaken his interest in liturgical art; the Benedictines' enthusiasm for the arts

Still today, dePaola's spirituality runs deep, as evidenced by this delicate figure of Mary that graces one of the wall niches in his studio.

DePaola spent the late 1950s and early 1960s creating liturgical murals, this one in 1960 for St. Sylvester's Church in Graniteville, Vermont. Entitled *Christ's Entry into Jerusalem*, the piece was rendered in acrylic on wood and was five-by-twelve feet in dimension.

proved to be highly beneficial. For the next years, his artistic endeavors revolved around creating murals and church vestments. DePaola calls this phase his "Brief Period." He was "briefly in a monastery, briefly lived in France, briefly designed church vestments, and was even briefly married."[22] Traces of his religious art training can be found in the backgrounds of books such as *Francis, the Poor Man of Assisi, The Lady of Guadalupe, The Parables of Jesus,* and *The Clown of God.* Although most of his murals have been dismantled or painted over in the course of redecoration, several still can be found in the Glastonbury Monastery in Hingham, Massachusetts,[23] and at the Dominican Retreat House in Schenectady, New York.[24]

These years also could be called dePaola's "Restless Period": Following his brief time in Paris, he went to Boston to teach art at Newton College of the Sacred Heart; relocated to San Francisco, where he was named assistant professor of art at Lone Mountain College and where he received his Master of Fine Arts at the California College of Arts and

Crafts; returned to Boston as instructor of art at Chamberlayne Junior
College; and then moved to New Hampshire, where he held first the
position of designer and technical director in speech and theater at Colby-
Sawyer College, then that of associate professor of art, and later was
named artist-in-residence at New England College.[25]

Brought up Catholic, dePaola had found early delight in the church's
mysteries, liturgies of worship, and stories of saints. "Once, when I was
ten, I stayed for three continuous showings of the movie *The Song of
Bernadette*," he tells. "I was so transfixed by Bernadette's pure and simple
faith that I would probably still be there if my worried parents hadn't
tracked me down."[26]

As an adult he has grown away from the church, although, he says,
"Spirituality is still a strong driving force in my life." Anyone following
dePaola's work would surely agree. In *Books & Religion*, writer Mary
Zeman, an artist and educator interested in the spiritual growth of
children, comments that "[dePaola's] voice is that of a receptive man,

whose approach to his work betrays what Thomas Merton once described as the willingness of saints 'to answer the secret voice of God calling—to take a risk and venture by faith outside the reassuring and protective limits of our five senses.'"[27]

DePaola experienced this kind of receptivity in San Francisco. Group therapy sessions allowed him to get in touch with the child in himself. For some time he had felt his career as an illustrator reaching an impasse; his work, he feared, was becoming unimaginative, uncreative, as colorless as the fog outside his San Francisco window. "I had totally fallen for that old line 'Don't be childish' and I had smothered my childlikeness; I had to like that child again." In particular, dePaola credits a woman therapist who agreed to take her fee in pictures and through them helped him once again discover the childlike pleasure in his art—the intensity—that he had had as a youngster.

In addition, he found his Whitebird symbol. A priest friend was coming to dePaola's apartment for a "home liturgy" celebration for Pentecost, the feast of the Holy Spirit.[28] Each person attending was asked to contribute a poem or a song. DePaola said he chose a piece of music called "White Bird"[29] because the white bird is the symbol of the Holy Spirit. "I realized that white birds had shown up in my work, and I remembered that in mythology the white bird was the messenger between the gods and humans. I know I get my inspiration from a higher source, and what better symbol for an artist, especially for me?" Nestled in windows, flapping from eaves, the whitebird symbol continues to show up in his books. "It's my way," dePaola says, "of acknowledging the source of my talent." Whitebird has become the name of his company and appears, in abbreviated form, on his cars' license plates.

Nowhere, perhaps, do white birds play a greater role than in dePaola's Christmas celebrations. The artist's love of the holiday is well known. For many years, holiday book buyers across the country could look forward to a new dePaola book each Christmas, and locally, friends and neighbors anticipated a holiday party in dePaola's home—a tradition he gave up because of pressing publication deadlines. His personal celebration for a season that he holds "in quiet awe as a time for contemplating life's mysteries and wonders" has a deeper effect.[30] In early December, Christmas folk-art pieces; thousands of tiny lights; fragrant greens; votive candles; and Christmas cactus, poinsettia, and amaryllis plants begin to fill the house.

As Christmas nears, trees inside and out are trimmed with lights and trinkets (many of them white birds), and twinkling luminarias add an extra fillip on the snow-filled deck and patio. The in-house trees are

At Christmastime, folk-art pieces, candles, and poinsettias intermingle, bringing a delight of color to dePaola's home.

artistic masterpieces, decorated from top to bottom. The ornaments include gifts from friends, purchases from dePaola's wide-ranging travels (he once bought out a shop's whole supply of gilded stars on the island of Bali), self-made ornaments, and creations from Midwest of Cannon Falls[31] (unfortunately no longer available) based on characters from *Country Angel Christmas.*

21 ♥

The bold colors of Christmas offer striking contrast to the white walls in dePaola's home, which, he claims, become the perfect canvas to celebrate his favorite of all holidays. He traces his love of Christmas back to his childhood. "I was three or four, and we still lived in a rented apartment. My father had a make-believe fireplace. I can still see it—covered with red crepe paper, with a fake log and a red electric lightbulb. 'That's where Santa comes,' my father told me. When we moved to Fairmount Avenue, we had a real chimney and real fireplace. My father put blue lights in all the windows. I was very impressed. During World War II we had blackouts and had to be careful of using lights, but when peace came and we could once more put lights in every window at Christmastime, I was delighted. When I got older I created a life-size Nativity set on our lawn. Every year I added more carolers, choirboys, angels, all the way through art school."

Even after he left home and didn't have much money, dePaola found inexpensive ways to decorate for Christmas. "I read that in medieval times people decorated with roses and apples, so I made hundreds of tissue-paper roses, some of which I still have. My parents often had huge parties during the holidays, and often I do too; on Christmas Day, sometimes twenty people or more, including my sisters' children and grandchildren, celebrate with me. Years ago, I read something that said Christmas is when 'the invisible becomes the visible,' and I thought that was a wonderful thing to say about Christmas—as well as something for an artist to keep in mind. Those words have stayed with me through the years."[32]

DePaola and his mother—in a mock depiction of Grant Wood's *American Gothic*, 1979.

In 1962, while teaching at Newton College of the Sacred Heart, dePaola garnered good reviews from his several one-man shows at Boston's The Botolph Group,[33] featuring his contemporary religious art. This early acclamation might have led him on an entirely different career path. However, his desire to become an illustrator had not gone away, and he decided to work out his teaching schedule so that he could live in New York—and be closer to the publishing community.

Through a series of coincidences, dePaola met Florence Alexander, an art representative, who became his agent and an influential force in his professional life.[34] "Florence," dePaola says, "created my career for me. She made me work very hard and take all kinds of funny little jobs and get my name out there. I owe a tremendous amount to her."[35] When then Coward-McCann editor-in-chief Alice Torrey decided to publish a physical science series[36] for young readers using a visual picture book approach, she hired Bernice Kohn (later Hunt) as the series editor. It was Kohn's idea to launch the series with two titles, one by a known artist and one by a new talent. She went to Alexander's office looking for an unknown illustrator; Alexander recommended dePaola. After perusing his portfolio, Kohn signed him up to illustrate *Sound*, which she herself had written under the pseudonym Lisa Miller. Later that year, dePaola illustrated *Wheels,* the third book in the series.

Following his return from San Francisco and his breakthrough to "the child within," as dePaola calls it, books rolled off the presses in quick succession. He illustrated eight books in 1973, four of which he wrote, including *Nana Upstairs & Nana Downstairs* and *"Charlie Needs a Cloak."* In 1974 he could count three finished publications; there were six in 1975, and nine in 1976. The banner year was surely 1977: DePaola produced artwork for fourteen titles, three that he wrote himself. At long last his dream of being a children's book illustrator was coming true. While reviewers hailed him as a "new talent" on the children's book scene, for dePaola it was the culmination of long, hard years of trying to get a foothold in the children's publishing world. These vividly remembered frustrations are one of the reasons dePaola so treasures his home and his Whitebird barn and studio.

Though fame and fortune no longer elude him, their extent, he admits, often baffles him. When asked to comment about the deeper meanings of his books, the usually exuberant, rarely shy dePaola admits that he finds it difficult to discuss the intricacies of his own work. He prefers the format that he uses to "talk" with children—the simple words and pictures on the page. What better place to begin than with his autobiographical stories.

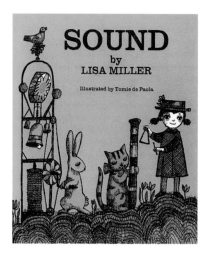

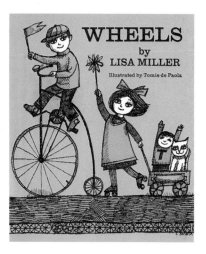

The covers of dePaola's first information books depict his early sense of design, penchant for whimsy, and ability to connect with children.

"Tommy knew he wanted to be an artist when he grew up.
He drew pictures everywhere he went." *The Art Lesson*

# Autobiographical Tales

On a television in dePaola's studio, pictures from old family movies (now transferred to video) often flicker across the screen, bringing images of the artist-author's family to life. His father, an ardent photographer and also a home-movie buff, rarely let a birthday party, summer picnic at the beach, Christmas festivity, or any family gathering go by without recording it on film. The great-grandparents, grandparents, parents, siblings, and other relatives who once so readily posed for the senior dePaola's camera now inhabit his son's stories, radiating warmth and believability.

DePaola, the recipient of these family treasures, says that these old home movies provide him with laughs and memories; it is obvious they furnish inspirational grist for his ever-active, creative mind. Evidence of the films' and photos' influence crops up in his books in several ways: In *Nana Upstairs & Nana Downstairs,* the protagonist's father is seen in the background with a home movie camera; in *Tom* and in *The Baby Sister,* photographic-style drawings identify the characters; in *The Art Lesson,* his photographer cousins make a cameo appearance; and in *Flicks,* a boy enjoys five "silent films" at the local movie theater. In a more general manner, his father's old movies reconnect dePaola with his past and act as a memory check for the background details that give such warm ambience to his illustrations. And while the artist has an acute recollection about events of his childhood, viewing these

Tommy's warm relationships with his grandparents, Nana Fall-River in *The Baby Sister*, ABOVE, and Tom in *Tom*, BELOW, reverberate naturally out of dePaola's astute visual depictions.

films and photos can't help but solidify the relatives' images as he works to capture their identities and likenesses in his artwork.

Whatever the source, dePaola's wonderful assortment of Irish and Italian relatives arrives on the page richly arrayed in costume, expression, and personality. Reading dePaola's autobiographical books is akin to getting to know the family—some sadness and pain show through, but love abounds. He contends that turning his childhood joys and traumas into stories delivers a core of reality that children can relate to and allows himself, as the writer, the opportunity for fictional invention.

DePaola the child is, of course, the focus of these stories. Readers meet him most often as the character Tommy—although sometimes he appears under other monikers. Tommy made his debut in *Nana* in 1973; then, after a sixteen-year absence, he returned in three titles (*The Art Lesson, Tom,* and *The Baby Sister*). In between, dePaola continued drawing upon his childhood experiences, veiling himself under other character names. He is Bobby in *Now One Foot, Now the Other*; Joey in *Watch Out for the Chicken Feet in Your Soup*; Andy in *Andy, That's My Name*; and Oliver in *Oliver Button Is a Sissy*. His return to using Tommy as a character name signifies, perhaps, an increased ease with his childhood self and a willingness to share that person directly with young readers. In offering children the opportunity to experience his real-life situations, dePaola lets his own vulnerability surface. Few children's authors are disposed to do so in the guise of story.

While dePaola's autobiographical stories focus on events, which pivot the stories' action, the underlying emotional issues are what tug at the heart. Deceptively simple, his books often contain layers of meaning. He deftly wraps the pleasure of an understanding teacher, the distressful death of a grandparent, the importance of a name, the arrival of a new sibling in the comforting cocoon of story. As these incidents unfold, young readers gain satisfaction from seeing the littlest (themselves) rising to face the adult world. At the same time, adults enjoy the stories from the vantage point of both the children they once were and the adults they have become. It is to dePaola's credit that he is able to encompass both audiences.

In 1973, when the first of his autobiographical tales appeared, dePaola had been illustrating children's books for eight years. And although at the time he could list thirty-some books in his illustration portfolio, he had authored only a few. This situation changed dramatically with the publication of *Andy, That's My Name* and *Nana Upstairs & Nana Downstairs,* both in that same year.

*Andy,* which deals on the surface with words and letters, has emotional roots in the author's feelings about the importance of names. His own first name involves an interesting story. While pregnant, dePaola's mother, sure her soon-to-be-born baby would be a boy, decided on the name Thomas. During a conversation with her cousin, the popular 1930s vocalist Morton Downey, she joked that the baby's heavy activity in the womb convinced her that "Thomas" would be a dancer; Downey supposedly replied that "he will have to spell it differently if he is going to be famous." This family story was repeated many times over, and while in high school, dePaola did, indeed, begin using his unusual spelling. "Tomie" has become so well known in children's literature circles and with children that several years ago, dePaola began signing simply "Tomie" (complete only when it contains a heart) when autographing books. He admits, however, that the spelling, along with varied pronunciations of his last name, has resulted in endless versions, many amusing situations, and a lot of frustrations. (Tomie is pronounced like Tommy, the character in his books; dePaola is pronounced daPowla, accent on the Pow.)

The flap copy for *Andy,* written at the time of publication (1973), states that the book is "a special treat for children just mastering reading

DePaola's 1973 use of dialogue balloons on the book's cover, LEFT, and title page, OVER, was highly innovative for its time.

27

While the boy and the four block letters spelling out his name constitute the general makeup of these three images, it is the little boy's changing posture, tilt of head, and facial expressions that energize the pages.

skills." It makes no mention of the story's possibility as a vehicle to foster self-esteem or to emphasize the importance of a child's name, both significant in classrooms of the 1990s. The book was conceptualized on a drive from Cambridge to Boston one night after work, when dePaola visualized a little boy on the street with a wagonload of huge alphabet blocks, an A, an N, a D, and a Y. According to Ellen Roberts, the editor for *Andy,*[1] "dePaola 'wrote' the book in a flash of inspiration, without ever taking his hands off the steering wheel. The execution, of course, took longer as he worked to make each spread logical and exciting. But his understanding of the principles of story and pictures brought him the concept in a sudden stroke of genius."

The title page arrangement, an example of dePaola's early sense of design and interest in a book's entire look, places Andy atop the letters A-N-D-Y. The author's name, as though being announced by the boy, is seen in a balloon over Andy's head, while the subtitle, *That's My Name,* appears in parentheses beneath the large letters. DePaola traces the idea to a graphic treatment he once saw used in an old film title.

Told entirely through pink-and-brown-shaded pictures and dialogue balloons, the story follows young Andy as he carts the letters A-N-D-Y

to a group of older children in the hope of joining their play. Instead, they grab the letters and make a variety of words, shutting him out of their fun. A disgruntled Andy finally gathers up his letters, saying, "I may be little, but I'm very important," and leaves. The final spread, echoing the title page, finds him on top of the letters; now, however, he is curled up protectively around his name, fast asleep. Humor as well as an understanding of a child's inner feelings envelop this simple concept book, making it more than it seems at first glance.

Clipped from an old family home movie, these photographs show the real Nana Downstairs and Nana Upstairs, ABOVE, and Nana Downstairs with young Tomie, FAR RIGHT, which dePaola has parlayed into well-known fictional characters.

Published later that same year, *Nana Upstairs & Nana Downstairs* has a direct connection to dePaola's life and is his first truly autobiographical book. In the story, young Tommy eagerly visits his grandmother (Nana Downstairs) and his feeble great-grandmother (Nana Upstairs), who is confined to her bed on the second floor. He happily watches Nana Downstairs bake a cake and comb her long, white hair into a bun, and then lovingly shares candy mints and stories with Nana Upstairs.

When Nana Upstairs dies, Tommy is devastated. Comfort arrives in the form of a falling star that Tommy witnesses late one night; his mother tells him, "Perhaps that was a kiss from Nana Upstairs." The final page reveals a grown-up Tommy, remembering Nana Downstairs, also now deceased. Seeing another falling star, he thinks, *Now you are both Nana Upstairs*. The well-conceived ending is an endearing tribute to his two Nanas from both the real Tomie and his fictional counterpart. This fast-forward-to-the-future technique, one dePaola also nimbly employs

This same scene from dePaola's 1973 *Nana Upstairs & Nana Downstairs*, FAR LEFT, and from his re-illustrated 1998 rendition, LEFT, display the subtle differences that line and color can bring to an image.

in *The Art Lesson,* gives readers a glimpse into dePaola as an adult and sends a message about growing older and the cycles of life.

To give artistic balance to both the sad and the uplifting aspects of the story, the artist chose subdued hues of umber and rose, highlighted with black lines and soft shading. The framing of each page with a scrolled design conveys the impression of old scalloped-edged photographs of the period and results in a harmonious connection between pictures and story, which no doubt has contributed to the book's early and continued popularity.

A sign of the importance of *Nana Upstairs & Nana Downstairs* to readers and to dePaola was the re-release of the title in 1998, for the book's twenty-fifth anniversary. Because his editor Margaret Frith,[2] and dePaola himself, considered *Nana* to be pivotal to the autobiographical grouping, the decision was made to give the "new" book a similar trim size to *The Art Lesson, The Baby Sister,* and *Tom,* and to recast it in full color.[3]

When he began to draw in preparation for the color, however, dePaola found that he needed to alter the line work as well, which provided a unique opportunity and a great challenge. As dePaola notes in the book's afterword, "It was not easy to re-illustrate the book in full color. It was hardly a matter of 'colorizing' or coloring in. My drawing style has changed subtly over time, so twenty-five years later I have approached *Nana Upstairs & Nana Downstairs* as a completely new book. It was important for me to retain the nostalgic feeling of the original, and I did this mostly with the use of soft color. Creating this art was as emotional

In a deeply poignant rendering, dePaola starkly but effectively portrays Tommy's sadness and disbelief over the death of his beloved great-grandmother in *Nana Upstairs & Nana Downstairs.*

an experience for me now as it was then." His efforts, especially the gentle colors to retain the atmosphere, have been successful; in updating the art, he has lost none of the story's sensitivity.

In the new illustrations, the artist's subtle changes bring more intimacy to the pictures. For example, backgrounds are texturized, pushing the images forward; the furniture is given a smooth shine, making the pictures less busy; and the characters' expressions are refined. An interesting connection can be found in the use of a large, teal-colored wing chair where Tommy is told of Nana Upstairs's death; undoubtedly, it is the same one that plays a role in *The Baby Sister.* The earlier book's cover art has been moved to the back of the jacket. Then, a clever manipulation of graphics happens. An original inside image shows Tommy's father making a home movie with brother Buddy holding the light, with the focus of the camera being Tommy and his two Nanas. The threesome, enlarged and set in a cameo shape, now warmly grace the book's new dust jacket.

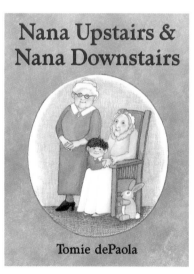

An embracing three-generational portrayal from the first edition has been lifted from the book's interior, effectively forming the image for the new dust jacket.

Another family allusion worth noting is a reference to his grandfather Tom, whom dePaola has featured in two different books: *Now One Foot, Now the Other,* published in 1981, and, some twelve years later, a book called, simply, *Tom.*

Two building-block episodes in *Now One Foot, Now the Other* supply poignant scenes between Bob and Bobby.

While dePaola was a child, he and his Irish grandfather enjoyed a special relationship, which clearly emerges in both titles. In *Now One Foot, Now the Other*, the young protagonist is Bobby and Grandfather is Bob—a more elderly and much feebler man than in *Tom*—but their real-life closeness shines through the fictional framework. Bob encourages toddler Bobby to walk by telling him, "Now one foot, now the other," a message that Bobby repeats some years later to his grandfather when he needs to relearn to walk after suffering from a stroke.

DePaola effectively ties the alternating story situations (the old helping the young, the young helping the old) together through a simple game of playing blocks. Described the first time, the game is a straightforward part of the story line; later it becomes a poignant memory that helps Bob on his road to recovery. Throughout the book, dePaola places the characters up front on the page and limits background detail, giving drama to the portrayals. Again, color is put to good use—shading effectively enhances the emotions, and the well-thought-out perspectives draw viewers in. The repeated images of Bob and Bobby in various time frames increase readers' familiarity with the two, and a slumped Bobby at his bedridden grandfather's door gives particular credibility to the boy's unease and unhappiness with Bob's deterioration.

From the opening lines, readers will sense their affection: "Bobby was named after his best friend, his grandfather, Bob. When Bobby was just a baby, his grandfather told everyone, 'Bobby will be three years old before he can say Grandpa, so I'm going to have him call me Bob.' And 'Bob' was the first word Bobby said." An interesting corollary is found in *Tom,* which begins: "'We're named after each other, Tommy. That's why I want you to call me Tom instead of Grandpa.' So Tommy did."

Gestures of the body and face provide keys to changing relationships as Bob teaches Bobby to walk, TOP LEFT; as Bobby grasps the effects of his grandfather's stroke, ABOVE; and as Bobby, LEFT, becomes the pillar for Bob's rehabilitation.

In *Tom*, the basement furnace room furnishes a warm setting as his grandfather Tom tells real stories about himself as a little boy, and some that he made up.

In *Tom*, Tommy's Irish grandfather, who owned a butcher shop, tells great stories, "some about himself when he was a little boy, and some that he made up. (Tommy loved those the best.)" Then one day Tom teases Tommy into planting chicken heads to grow a "chicken bush." The impatient Tommy can't wait for them to grow and digs them up to check their progress—which, Tom tells him, destroys their chance of survival. DePaola, who enjoyed this kind of humorous banter with his own grandfather, eases it into the story and accompanying pictures with aplomb. Another funny incident occurs when Tom shows Tommy how chicken feet tendons can be manipulated so that the feet seemingly move on their own. Intrigued, Tommy takes two chicken feet home, and after scouring them ("They were kind of smelly"), brightening the claws with red nail polish, and practicing to make them open and close, he takes them to school. His trick scares his schoolmates and gives Tommy many a laugh, but it also lands him in a heap of trouble.

In visually re-creating these incidents, dePaola fashions images ripe with humor. He gives the boy a self-confident air as he "attacks" his friends with moving chicken feet, building tension toward the boy's inevitable downfall. And when the teacher inadvertently becomes a victim and the principal sends Tommy home with a note—"Tommy is not allowed to bring chicken feet to school ever again"—readers will identify with the chastised boy. Only when Tom, with a big wink, tells him, "We'll just have to think of something else to do. Don't you think?" is Tommy mollified. "Having a grandfather who got you into *that* kind of trouble at school," dePaola says with a chuckle, "was, actually, wonderful!"

Action and humor combine when Tommy successfully frightens Jeannie with moving chicken claws painted with red nail polish in *Tom*.

From *Tom*, an illustrated version of a photograph of Tom and baby Tommy adds a sense of nostalgia.

"Hi, baby," Tommy whispers.

The dePaola photography connection is well employed here with a snapshot-style picture of Tom and baby Tommy on the title page and a second one of Tom and Tommy, at the time of the story, on the back jacket. Presented in sepia tones, the pictures supply an appropriately old-fashioned flavor and inject a subtle time line to the ongoing dePaola story. They also emphasize the existing affection between grandfather and grandson.

In *The Baby Sister*, dePaola expands on this photograph-framing structure. In this sweet story, a young boy's excitement about the upcoming arrival of a new baby ripples through the pages. Tommy, who already has an older brother, asks his mother for a sister with "a red ribbon in her hair." To help get ready for the baby's arrival, Tommy paints pictures for the baby's room, whispers "Hi, baby," to his mother's tummy, and in his nightly prayers repeats his petition, asking God to "send me a baby sister with a red ribbon in her hair." When his mother goes to the hospital, Tommy's visiting outspoken Italian grandmother, Nana Fall-River,[4] stays on, instead of Tommy's hoped-for Aunt Nell.[5] An unhappy Tommy, missing his mother, refuses to eat and mopes around the house. However, the sight of Mom waving from the hospital window changes his disposition; he goes home and flings himself into Nana's arms with the words "Let's be friends." And indeed, when his mother and baby sister arrive home, it is Nana herself who places the warm bundle in Tommy's lap and pulls back the blanket, revealing baby Maureen with a perky red bow in her hair.

The story's pacing is well managed: Pictures appear in a variety of sizes and maintain the story's flow while delivering the necessary continuity. The large, teal-colored wing chair, for instance, provides the setting for several important events in the story and offers emotional focus. It's where Tommy imagines he and Aunt Nell will read stories together; it's where he unhappily huddles while missing his mother; it's what he hides behind at the homecoming (hoping his mother will ask for him—she does); and it's where he finds a comforting place to hold and meet his long-awaited baby sister.

Tommy's encircling hands and the baby's upreaching fingers affectionately link the two siblings in the closing image of *The Baby Sister*.

Tomie and Maureen, in 1945.

Tomie and Maureen, in 1996.

DePaola bathes his backgrounds in mottled colorings of peach, soft yellow, and bluish green; casts his characters' clothing in brighter shades for contrast; and adds sturdy lines to effect strong facial expressions. The resulting combination provides an upbeat look for an upbeat story. And in light of the many sibling stories where the baby is not, or at least not initially, welcomed by the older child, this book can serve as a nice alternative.

By opting to use color rather than accessories for the background, the artist takes this highly personal story to an Everychild plane, which gives it wider appeal. Nevertheless, the book's dedication, "For my sister, Maureen," as well as the biographical information and a photograph of a young dePaola with his real-life sister on the back jacket flap, ground the story in reality. DePaola undoubtedly delved into the family's photograph collection to find this childhood memento. Then, not to leave anyone out, he created two pages of "snapshots" that begin the story, with the caption "Tommy had a mother, a father, two grandmothers, one grandfather, lots of aunts and uncles, an older brother, Buddy, and a dog named Tootsie. . . ."

Queried about the line between fact and fiction in this story, dePaola relates that all the basic incidents happened: his request for a baby sister with a red ribbon in her hair, the unwelcome appearance of Nana Fall-River, the "Let's be friends" scene, and the depositing of baby Maureen in his arms. He says, however, that he made some alterations for the sake of story. For instance, he telescoped the time frame (in those days, mothers were kept in the hospital for as long as ten days) and injected the "chicken pox is going around" line as a reason why Tommy couldn't go to the hospital. That explanation would be easier for today's children to understand, he felt, than the "No children allowed" rule of 1930s hospitals. Modifications of this kind are why dePaola calls these books "autobiographical fiction" and why, in part, he uses Tommy rather than Tomie for the protagonist's name.

Brought to fruition in *The Baby Sister*, the seed of dePaola's childhood anticipation of his real-life sister's birth first surfaced in another of his books, published some seventeen years earlier. *Flicks*, a wordless book, is made up of five short "silent movies," each one with a surprise ending. To set the stage, dePaola features an Art Deco movie theater on the front of a wraparound jacket, with movie-going children studying the "Now Playing" and "Coming Attractions" placards on the theater wall. Front matter shows the children buying tickets; handing them to the ticket taker; filing into the theater, popcorn in hand; and settling into their seats. As the individual "flicks" play out, the reader views them over the audience's heads, which appear in silhouette, making this going-to-the-movies experience ever the more realistic.

One of the stories is entitled "The New Baby." Rendered, as they all are, in black line drawings textured with shadings of gray, this vignette depicts a young boy happily gathering together a baby bonnet and baby bottles and decorating a bassinet for a new occupant—in this case, as the last image shows, a somewhat startled-looking kitten. The story seems an obvious precursor to *The Baby Sister,* or at the very least, an indicator of the importance Maureen's arrival had in dePaola's boyhood life.

While the humorous situations depicted in *Flicks* are imagined, the venue in which they are set places this book most appropriately within dePaola's autobiographical tales. For example, one of the young boys entering the movie theater wears a large *T* on his shirt, the only child to have a letter designation.

Films were an exciting part of dePaola's childhood. As he relates, "I remember every detail of those Saturday-morning movies I went to as a kid. Standing in line for the ticket, the smell and sound of corn popping,

DePaola's love of surprise surfaces in *Flicks*, where, after much tender preparation, the new arrival turns out to be—a kitten.

racing up the stairs to the balcony, and feeling my way down the steps to the front row in the darkness. And then—the magic began. The music, the squeaky, jerky motion of the curtain opening as the picture played over it, and the stars who filled the screen and my heart. Mickey Mouse and Mae West were my favorites."[6] It is no surprise, then, to find a dedication page honoring Mickey, Mae, Shirley (Temple), and Minnie (Mouse), with small head shots.

The Hollywood heroes of dePaola's childhood (*Flicks*), ABOVE, and Oliver's dance routine (from *Oliver Button Is a Sissy*), FAR RIGHT, exemplify the artist's effective use of the filmstrip sequence.

In only two of his autobiographical tales, *Oliver Button Is a Sissy* and *The Art Lesson*, has dePaola put himself prominently at center stage; in the others, a family member shares the spotlight or the protagonist is part of an ensemble. Published in 1979, *Oliver Button* was formatted and styled in tune with the original versions of *Nana Upstairs & Nana Downstairs* and *Now One Foot, Now the Other*. Illustrated in two colors, with backgrounds void of detail, *Oliver Button Is a Sissy* focuses, like *The Art Lesson*, on a central character in a specific situation. The young protagonist, who would rather draw or tap-dance than play sports, is taunted by his classmates until his dance performance shows that he really does have talent.

Teasing and hurtful taunts distress young Oliver, RIGHT and TOP RIGHT, but like dePaola, the resilient Oliver dances into the spotlight.

The plot, which pivots on a serious theme, is lightened with humor and made believable with individualized characters. Any child who has ever been teased by a classmate—for whatever situation—will relate to Oliver's dismay at having his tap shoes flung around the playground. And it is not only children who relate to this tale. Charles Massey, a New York theatrical manager, gave copies of the book to many of the performers who joined the cast of the musical *A Chorus Line* in its beginning years on Broadway.[7]

DePaola named his main character Oliver Button because, he says, he liked the way it sounded, but Oliver's problems, he admits, are ones he encountered in his own childhood. "I could spend hours drawing," dePaola says, "but I hated sports; nobody ever asked me to play on their ball team because I was so bad at it. But, like Oliver, I was a great tap dancer." DePaola's mother's premonition, in fact, has come true— her son learned to dance, and he has become famous.

By the time dePaola tackled the story of his confrontation with his first-grade art teacher in *The Art Lesson,* his skills as storyteller and illustrator had grown. Characters are fleshed out in expression and appearance, line work is brisker, colors are stronger, and backgrounds reflect a more definite sense of place. Written in 1989 in the midst of the growing market for picture books for older children, the story appeals to a wide range of readers. And by naming the protagonist Tommy, dePaola returned to the tradition begun in *Nana Upstairs & Nana Downstairs* of using incidents from his early years as a bridge to his storytelling.

Although the cataloging information[8] lists the book as fiction, the story is grounded thoroughly in dePaola's real life. The dedication, in fact, divulges that there was once an art teacher named Mrs. Beulah Bowers. In addition, sharp-eyed readers will find other clues: a picture on the wall of baby Maureen, and mention of Nana Fall-River; a small drawing of brother Joe (sister Judie had not been born); a scene of Tom and Nana at their meat counter; and an appearance of Tommy's father in his barber shop.

*The Art Lesson* overflows with Tommy's joy in the artistic process, seen here in this array of portraits.

The final spread depicts a grown-up Tommy at his drawing board, a bowl of popcorn at his side, revealing that Tommy and Tomie dePaola are one and the same. On the wall, readers will find images of the shepherd Charlie, Strega Nona, and Bill and Pete, as well as dePaola's signature image, the white bird.

*The Art Lesson* is more than just a vehicle to tell a family story. It is about a young boy whose drawing abilities have delighted his family for years but who finds his eager anticipation of school (and art classes) dimmed when he meets up with the regimentation of the teacher. Once more, dePaola's ability and willingness to build a story around a real-life experience give children the opportunity to reflect on their own school-centered emotions and concerns.

From the popcorn at his side to the familiar book figures on the wall, clues to the real Tomie dePaola abound in this final spread from *The Art Lesson*.

This warmth and merriment extends into dePaola's chapter-book series—26 Fairmount Avenue. Just as in his picture books, these stories are about growing up, following one's artistic muse, and, most importantly, keeping one's individuality, a theme that young readers will remember long after the last page is turned. Although dePaola addresses this theme of individuality in a variety of ways throughout his work, nowhere does he do it so thoughtfully as in the many religious books he has written and illustrated.

# The Beginnings of **26 Fairmount Avenue**

During his long tenure as a children's picture book artist and author, dePaola has visited hundreds of schools and talked with an even greater number of children after storytelling programs and in autographing lines. "Children have told me a lot over the years," the artist-author comments, "and I have discovered that the books they respond to most are the ones based on my own life." As these fans grow older, they beg for longer books, chapter books to accompany them into their middle grades. At first, dePaola rejected the idea: He had always considered himself first an artist and second a writer. However, as time went on, he began taking the children's continuing requests more seriously, and he discussed the possibilities of a chapter book series with his editor, Margaret Frith. With her encouragement (and some good-natured prodding from assistant Bob Hechtel, who had read many of these same requests from children in the thousands of letters dePaola receives), dePaola began, in 1997, the writing of *26 Fairmount Avenue,* the first title in the series of the same name, leading him into a new phase of his career.

Using his childhood address in Meriden, Connecticut, as the anchor, dePaola began to spin out childhood incidents, cast in an even stronger autobiographical mode than his picture books. Told in the first person, he is, at last, Tomie. The stories are also more complex. "It was a different writing experience," dePaola says. "After years of paring down text to the absolute essentials—necessary in a picture book—I could now use more words to tell my stories and incorporate episodes beyond the picture-book-crowd experience."

The first title begins with the 1938 hurricane that hit the coast of Connecticut when dePaola was four, and goes on to relate the family's move from their ground-floor apartment on Columbus Avenue in Meriden to the home they built at 26 Fairmount Avenue. His memories of that devastating storm go on to cover the commotion he made when seeing Disney's film *Snow White and the Seven Dwarfs* and the time when the burning of the undergrowth around their newly constructed house nearly set it ablaze.

DePaola alludes to some incidents readers may remember from earlier titles—being tied into a chair just like Nana Upstairs (*Nana Upstairs & Nana Downstairs*), and using the walls to draw murals of the family when their house was under construction (*The Art Lesson*)—but they are woven seamlessly into the bigger story. The greater part of the narrative is new material, which rings with typical dePaola zestiness that children will find funny, poignant, and appealing. Readers also will become reacquainted with other familiar family members such as Buddy, Tom, Nana Fall-River, and Nana Downstairs and meet new ones—Uncle Charles and his girlfriend Viva—and friends Carol Crane and Mickey Lynch.

While the books were still in the planning process, dePaola considered making them strictly textual, but feedback from friends, colleagues, and Frith convinced him otherwise. Now, lively black-and-white drawings peppered through the pages add visual support to the humorous and sometimes traumatic events. Although longer and more in-depth, the stories are signature dePaola to the core!

"Finally the rainbow of colored balls." *The Clown of God*

# Religious Books

Just as dePaola's autobiographical stories emanate from the wellspring of his personal life and background, so his religious books arise from his deep-felt spirituality. His early-childhood interest in saints and miracles, as well as his intrigue with contemporary liturgical art, which spurred him to enter the Vermont monastery, surface in the backgrounds of his books. "One of the reasons I became interested in doing books with spiritual themes," the author commented, "was because of the mythic quality of these stories."

A survey of his work in this genre reflects a wide interest: collections of Bible stories, biographies of saints and other biblical figures, individual tales surrounding holidays, concept board books for toddlers, and retellings of various religious legends. In a reply to a question concerning the decisions that go into pursuing a book on St. Francis, the Virgin Mary, or the Petook Easter legend, for example, the author conveys a long-felt concern that "these meaningful stories be available for all children in beautiful formats with well-appointed pictures." And while admitting to a strong interest in the necessary research, he is adamant that the story "appeal to the child."

Here, too, lies evidence of dePaola's versatility. For his holiday board books dePaola uses simple, direct, and unadorned pictures, clear shapes, and primary colors, which focus on the symbols of the occasion.

The biographies (*Patrick, Patron Saint of Ireland* and *Christopher, the*

*Holy Giant*) contain more sophisticated illustrations and more complex narratives—stretching minds and imaginations. The contrasting techniques present a fine example of how the artist conceives books with concern for the ways children process thoughts. He is ever mindful of the child's mind and the child's eye.

For example, in retelling the life of Ireland's patron saint, Patrick, which his Irish mother had prodded him to do for years, dePaola uses forceful lines; a varied mixture of greens, blues, and golds; and a highly stylized approach. Patrick's life unfolds through isolated events, linked through friezelike panels that concentrate on one incident per image. By choosing this method, the artist is able to keep the text simple, injecting the needed emotion into artwork that has been touched with Celtic symbols. The book closes with five legends, each with its own

illustrations. As in the main text, these stories are told without much detail, allowing the artwork to carry the drama. It is a very suitable portrayal for the life of this monastic man.

*Christopher, the Holy Giant* follows somewhat the same pattern, although because it is based on a single legend rather than on the entire life of a person, the telling is more cohesive. Colors are more vivid, and images, especially those of Christopher, are appropriately larger. Particularly compelling are the scenes of Christopher carrying the Christ Child across a stormy river. Derived from a fresco dePaola found on a column in the Basilica of San Petronius in Bologna, Italy, they bring power to the page: As a host of angels sing above, a struggling Christopher perseveres through swirling patterns of blue and green waves, with the Christ Child on his back.

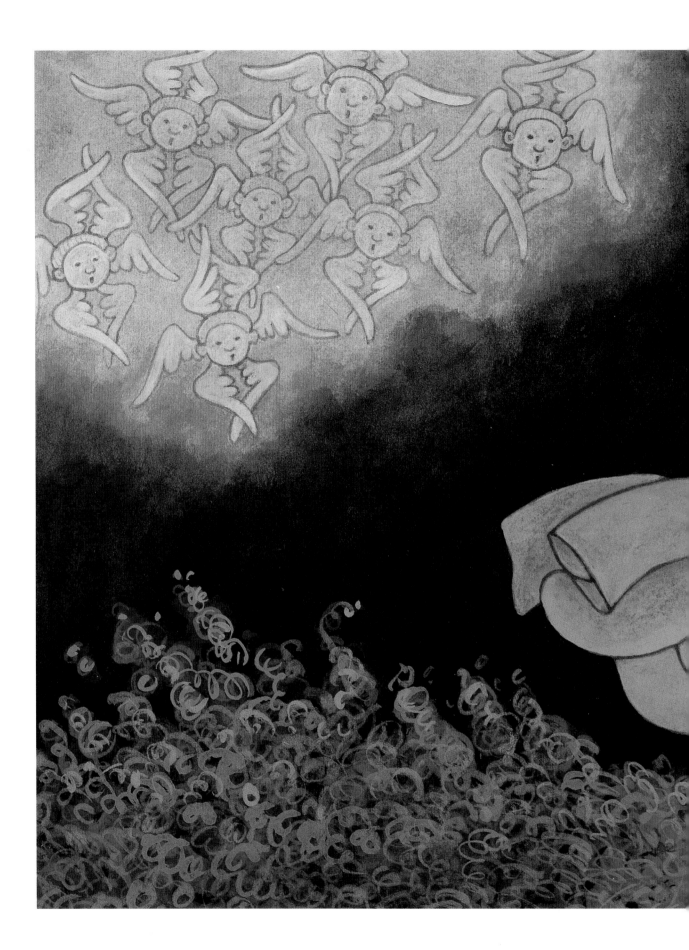

"The further he went, the higher the water rose and the heavier the child became." *Christopher, the Holy Giant*

In *The Little Friar Who Flew*, dePaola's use of frothy colors, white space, and playfulness expands the story's lighthearted spirit.

DePaola's first foray into stories about saints was *The Little Friar Who Flew*, playfully retold by Patricia Lee Gauch. The legend features the spontaneous levitations of an Italian friar, Joseph of Copertino, who lived between 1602 and 1663. Named a saint in 1767, Joseph became the patron saint of aviators in the twentieth century.[1]

In illustrating Joseph, whose joy in the natural world was the source of his ability to fly, dePaola effectively uses the page bottom as the base for the viewer's perspective. As the friar "flies" across white space, an illusion of Joseph's height results from how much of the image the reader sees at the bottom of the page—for example, the heads of sheep or the top of a church's dome. To extend this illusion and to balance the white space, dePaola places medieval towers or large trees at inner or outer margins. Using a straight-on perspective can be static if the action doesn't compensate; this is not a problem here, as Joseph's frolicsome antics continually focus the reader's attention. This theatrical effect surely can be traced to dePaola's one-time work as a set and costume designer.

A hundred years before Joseph took to the skies, a miracle of a different sort happened in Mexico. In *The Lady of Guadalupe,* a poor farmer named Juan Diego is singled out by the Mother of God to carry a message to the bishop, telling him to build a church in her honor. After Juan is dismissed twice by the bishop, the Lady tells him to return to the bishop and take the beautiful Castilian roses that have now appeared on the once-barren hilltop. Juan gives the bishop the roses, but what impresses the church father is the image of the Lady now imprinted on Juan's rough-fibered *tilma*. At last, he heeds her request and builds a church on the spot of the Lady's visitation.

In contrast to *The Little Friar Who Flew*, stronger lines and more solid shapes give a needed, more solemn look to *The Lady of Guadalupe*.

Soft changes of line and shading subtly alter the four portrayals of Mary in *Mary, the Mother of Jesus.*

DePaola celebrates this miracle in an oversize book that is rendered in the tradition of Mexican folklore. It was translated into a well-received Spanish edition with no change in format or size by Pura Belpré,[2] whose *The Tiger and the Rabbit, and Other Tales* was the second book dePaola illustrated. Holiday House publisher John Briggs thinks that it was possibly the first children's book to be issued in four editions simultaneously: an English-language edition in hardcover and paperback, and a Spanish-language edition in hardcover and paperback.[3]

An endnote elaborates on the story. Here, dePaola tells that Juan's woven fabric garment, called a *tilma*, hangs today in the church at Guadalupe, and although it is more than four hundred years old, it shows no sign of deterioration. Although it is now common to find source notes in folktales, dePaola may well be credited with starting, or at least with advancing, the trend.

The Mother of God in *The Lady of Guadalupe* seems to be a more mature woman—saddened, perhaps, by the world's woes and griefs that she witnesses from the heavens—than the Mary in *Mary, the Mother of Jesus.* In relating her time on earth, dePaola divides the story into chapters, depicting the incidents of Mary's life from birth to Ascension. Formal, single-page spreads are complemented by smaller, more symbolic images on the text pages. Mary's countenance subtly changes from shy bride to wondrous mother, to bereaved viewer at the Crucifixion, to receiver of the Holy Spirit, and finally to Holy Mother. The pastel colors take on denser hues at times, depending on what is being portrayed, adding richness to the story. Decorations include stars and doves, dePaola trademarks and familiar Christian symbols, as well as drawings of fruit.

In answer to a question about the puzzling image on the dust jacket of Mary holding an apple—a fruit usually associated with Eve in the Garden of Eden—dePaola cites a book on church symbolism that states that the apple is "sometimes given to the Virgin Mary, for it was her Son who took away the curse of sin."[4] It was a device that medieval painters often used, dePaola says. He, too, likes to include such devices in his art. "I am a stylized, not a realistic, painter, and I often use symbolic representations in my work." The artist points to *The Clown of God* as another example where, in the final pages, he includes a partial view of a window where none appeared before. The window, dePaola says, represents the clown's redemption, the release of his soul to the heavens.

The life of St. Francis of Assisi was one dePaola had wanted to explore for many years, and the celebration of the saint's eight hundredth birth anniversary (1982) seemed the perfect time.[5] In doing so, he returned (figuratively) to Italy, the setting for *The Little Friar,* judiciously taking into account that St. Francis lived five centuries before St. Joseph. While there are some similarities in the two Italian settings—red-tiled roofs and soft-colored building stones—the approach and style in each book are, appropriately, much different. In *Francis, the Poor Man of Assisi,* a biography dePaola both wrote and illustrated, rich paintings, executed in transparent inks, appear as full-page images on the right-hand side of each spread. The juxtaposed text on the left is set off with a large illuminated-style initial letter. At page bottom, a small vignette provides balance as well as additional detail for the larger picture, similar to the format used in *Mary, the Mother of Jesus,* without the illuminated letters.

In an endeavor to present the humble yet remarkable life of St. Francis, dePaola made two research trips to Italy (touched on in a foreword and in an afternote) to see where the monk carried on his mission and to study the frescoes of Francis and his companion, Sister Clare. But close examination of the illustrations discloses that while he obviously did his homework, his poignant visual descriptions result mainly from

In a well-balanced double-page presentation, dePaola places an illuminated letter at the text's beginning and a simple, symbolic design at page bottom, and elegantly portrays Francis as a young nobleman before his conversion in this pivotal meeting with a prophetic beggar. *Francis, the Poor Man Of Assisi*

RANCIS WAS ALWAYS IN TROUBLE. DRESSED LIKE A RAINBOW, HE RUSHED AROUND Assisi with his friends, eating, drinking, and having a good time.

Many a night, the good people of Assisi were awakened from a sound sleep by the noise of loud singing and guitar music.

Looking out their windows, they would catch a glimpse of a hat with a long red feather.

"Ah," they would say, "it is Francis again. Does he never sleep?"

One day, Francis was pushing through the noisy crowds in the little streets. All around him, the people were talking about war against the neighboring city of Perugia.

Suddenly a beggar stopped him. The beggar took off his tattered cloak and threw it on the ground, as if Francis were a prince and the cloak was a carpet for him to walk on.

"I have no coins," Francis said.

"I don't want any!" said the beggar. "I do this to honor you, for soon you will do great things which will be talked about until the end of the world."

A series of background arches
effectively center Francis's
dance movements as he
celebrates the "wonderful joy
of God" in long-ago Assisi.
*Francis, the Poor Man of Assisi*

a greater reach into his own artistic well. Characterization is deepened
through individualized facial expressions, fluid body movement, the tilt
of a head, and, particularly, the position of the hands. While his dots-
for-eyes, line-for-mouth technique was appropriate for many earlier,
more lighthearted titles, this insightful rendering is what the subject
demands, and dePaola clearly delivers. Even *The Lady of Guadalupe*,
where more fully realized character depictions can be seen, doesn't
project the pathos and jubilance found in the characters in *Francis*.

On the dust jacket, for example, the angle of the branches and
leaves, and the placement of the birds on one side and the still figure
of the man on the other force the eye to page center, where St. Francis's

graceful, expressive hands are frozen in mid-gesture. From the joy Francis emanates when he dances as a young beggar ("I am God's fool") to the radiant song that erupts from his pain-wracked body on his deathbed, dePaola captures the essence of this remarkably devoted man. DePaola often "borrows" from the masters—this time from Giotto. One need only look at Giotto's portrayal of St. Francis to see an intriguing resemblance in the positioning of the hands.[6]

One of the most profound and splendidly illustrated stories of dePaola's career, certainly of his earlier years, is *The Clown of God.* The beginnings of this book lodge in an old French tale, "Our Lady's Juggler," remembered from his childhood. In fact, he prepared a preliminary jacket before discovering that Barbara Cooney had previously illustrated that particular version.[7] His continued research eventually took him to a collection by Anatole France, and from there to a much earlier medieval source that had a "Mary's tale" as its basis. DePaola reshaped the story, adding a Christmas component, and infused it, especially through the illustrations, with an Italian setting.

Placing the story in Sorrento, at the beginning of the Renaissance, dePaola portrays an orphaned beggar boy named Giovanni, who happily entertains the market crowds with his juggling talents. When a passing theatrical troupe takes Giovanni under its wing, the boy eagerly goes with them. He puts on a clown face, attracting increasingly bigger crowds in each town with his tricks, until, a master of his art, he takes off on his own. Traveling the length and breadth of Italy, he mesmerizes the people by juggling sticks, plates, rings, and burning torches—always finishing with the "Sun in the Heavens," where balls of many colors, topped by a golden orb, flash and tumble rainbowlike into the sky.

One day Giovanni meets two monks on the road who tell him that his talent is a gift from God—that the founder of their order, Brother Francis (referring to St. Francis of Assisi), said that "if you give happiness to people, you give glory to God as well." Years pass, and Giovanni entertains well, but as he ages his hands become less nimble and his feats passé.

When his aging fingers cause him to drop the rainbow of balls, and people laugh, Giovanni vows to give up his juggling. He becomes a beggar once again and slowly heads back home to Sorrento. Arriving on a cold, dark night, he takes refuge in the monastery church of the Little Brothers of St. Francis and falls asleep. He awakens to music, blazing candlelight, and a procession of people laying gifts at the feet of the ancient and revered statue of the Lady and the Child: It is Christmas Eve. Later, after everyone has gone, Giovanni creeps close to the statue.

DePaola's cover for *The Clown of God* has its visual origins in a preliminary jacket for *Our Lady's Juggler*, a book never completed.

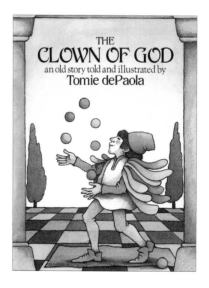

But Giovanni didn't hear or notice him.

"And now," said Giovanni, smiling at the face
of the Child, "First the red ball, then the orange...

Although he has no gift to leave for the Christ Child, he is moved by the solemn expression on the Child's face. Remembering that he "used to make people smile," Giovanni puts on his clown face once more and begins to juggle. Up fly his rings and sticks, plates and balls; never has he performed the "Sun in the Heavens" so well. But suddenly his poor heart gives out and Giovanni falls to the floor. When the brothers arrive, they find the old man dead, but the golden ball lies securely in the Christ Child's hand and a smile touches his face.

This unsophisticated tale offers intellectual stimulation and emotional engagement while providing a simple message about valuing one's own talents. The story and the art, however, are far more complex. The text has the multiple facets of a good biography, and the illustrations encompass strategic use of page composition, color, texture, character portrayal, and pace. They also show, as do many dePaola books, the decided influence of such early Renaissance painters as Fra Angelico, Giotto, Botticelli, and Piero della Francesca. Subtly fashioned details give dimension and provide backbone to the story's inherent dramatic power.

The title page nicely sets the scene. Villagers gather around an open-air, festooned stage on which a masked clown holds high a tambourine. On the backdrop a rainbow of ribbons announces the book's title and author. In the beginning pages, pastel colors shaded with earthy tones give texture and are balanced with white space, creating a lighthearted,

open look. Later, when things go poorly for Giovanni, white space disappears. Darkly clouded skies, deep-toned hills and trees, and gray cathedral walls signal a change of mood and the coming of the story's climax. They also adroitly serve as an emotional counterpoint to the colorful final image, when readers see the golden ball in the hands of the smiling Christ Child.

Architectural, geographical, and costume details help anchor the story in time and place. For example, dePaola presents varied scenes with the words "Up and down Italy [Giovanni] traveled." In one, country

In *The Clown of God*, dePaola's final image of a Madonna and Child, who holds a round object symbolizing the world, FAR RIGHT, has ties to early Christian artworks, such as this fifteenth-century alabaster statue in the British Museum, and to a painting dePaola created in the early 1950s.

peasants with hoes and bales of straw watch the juggler perform; in another, Venetian gondoliers ply their boats in the foreground. DePaola, who has long been cognizant of the concept of diversity, included a black gondolier after finding a similar image in Carpaccio's *Miracle of the Relic of the True Cross*.[8] Borrowing (but not copying) from the great masters is something dePaola does freely. This borrowing not only adds richness to the illustrations, but it gives adults excellent touchstones to lead children from the picture books they know to the great art that they might one day see in museums around the world.

As the story develops, the reader's attention focuses on the protagonist. At the start, Giovanni appears quite small and is, at times, just a figure in the crowd. Later, as his talents grow, he takes a more prominent place on the page. Then, when he first performs the "Sun in the Heavens" trick, he appears center stage, the crowd relegated to the periphery. When the story ends and Giovanni falls at the foot of the statue, arm reaching out, dePaola places him low on the page, his juggling accoutrements spilled around him, the walls of the cathedral arching above—a fine composition that delivers the dramatic impact the scene demands.

In 1992, dePaola once again used a clown as the focal point for a story—a Christmas tale that also embraces the theme of valuing one's own talents.

"The baby animals formed a pyramid. Jingle gave each of them a candle, and there in the middle of the square stood a living Christmas tree." *Jingle, the Christmas Clown*

# Christmas Stories

*Jingle, the Christmas Clown,* an original story, is set in Italy and, like *The Clown of God,* includes a traveling theatrical troupe—this time Il Circo Piccolo, the Little Circus. As the story opens, the troupe arrives in a small village, ready to entertain on Christmas Eve. When they learn that the village has fallen on hard times and that the elderly, the only ones still living there, have no money for the performance, the circus goes on to the city. But the baby animals, too tired to travel anymore, are left behind in young Jingle's care. When Jingle sees the villagers' sadness at missing the annual Christmas celebration, he takes matters into his own hands.

One of the villagers, Donna Chiara, makes costumes, while Jingle and the baby animals, after they've rested, rehearse. Jingle coaches the lion and tiger cubs to jump through hoops, the four monkey babies to swing from trapezes, and the young elephant and donkey to trot in circles with the two puppies on their backs, while he "tumbled better than he had ever tumbled before." For a finale, the entire ensemble forms a pyramid and, with lighted candles, becomes a living Christmas tree. As the villagers gasp in wonder, an angel appears overhead and golden stars flutter down through the skies. One attaches itself over the young clown's heart.

These two clown books, *Jingle* and *The Clown of God,* offer good contrasts in dePaola's methods of foreshadowing as he prepares children for the story ahead. In *The Clown of God,* readers meet Giovanni as a boy and follow him into manhood and death. The juggler's sacrifice and coming death are noted in several ways: careful pacing of the story and a measured cadence to the text; a cresting of Giovanni's career in the first half of the book, signaling that something—undoubtedly tragic—is going to happen; and changes in body expression, background detail, and color tones.

*Jingle,* a more lighthearted tale, takes place over a relatively short span of time and in one location. It deals not with an entire life but with a single incident. The antics of the baby animals, even in a time of distress, amuse, and the villagers are pictured as kindly. Though readers may not know exactly how Jingle and his friends will fare, there is no sense of impending doom. In keeping with that mood, the text trips quickly along and the jewel-like colors almost sparkle.

In both cases, a message is there for the taking, but it is subordinate to the tale. Readers will focus on Giovanni and Jingle; it is through their actions that dePaola's belief in the joy of giving comes through.

DePaola acknowledges that Christmas is his favorite holiday and has been important to him since his childhood, when his home was filled with "lots and lots of lights, many good things to eat, and crowds

DePaola's pleasure in Christmas shines through both the solemnity he injects in *The Friendly Beasts,* RIGHT, and the fancifulness he infuses in *Country Angel Christmas,* FAR RIGHT.

of friends and relatives." It is much the same today: In December his New Hampshire home boasts numerous Christmas trees, hundreds of candles, and decorations from his many worldwide travels. This love affair with Christmas has wound its way into a variety of Christmas books: funny tales (*Santa's Crash-Bang Christmas*), illustrated versions of carols (*The Friendly Beasts*), collections (*Tomie dePaola's Book of Christmas Carols*), various retellings of the Christmas story (*The Christmas Pageant* and *The First Christmas: A Pop-up Book*), and poignant stories that often have a profound message beyond their Christmas theme (*Pages of Music, Country Angel Christmas,* and *Jingle, the Christmas Clown*).

In *The Christmas Pageant,* dePaola's love of Christmas merges with his love of theater. To tell the familiar biblical story, he chooses simple, straightforward words that even a young child can understand, and supplies a stage setting for the unfolding plot. Children in costumes (donned on the title page), sheep on wheels, and angels and stars hanging from rafters play out the Christmas Eve story. It is all very childlike and effective.

*Tomie dePaola's Book of Christmas Carols,* on the other hand, represents the more regal side of the artist's oeuvre: luminescent colors resembling stained glass; stylized folk objects; a formal balance of text, art, and white space; and three gatefolds that not only bring a linear pageantry to those pages but carry a sense of elegance through the whole book. *The First Christmas: A Pop-up Book,* another perennial dePaola Christmas favorite, also demonstrates the artist's interest in trying different techniques and working in new ways—and, perhaps, allows him an opportunity to wrap his favorite of holidays in a bright and festive package.

Two other Christmas books, *The Night Before Christmas* and *An Early American Christmas,* deserve special scrutiny not only for their artistic merit, but also for the connections dePaola makes that enrich each work.

In illustrating Clement Moore's *The Night Before Christmas,* dePaola set his version in the 1840s, an appropriate and fascinating choice, considering the poem's history.[1] Moore, a professor of Greek and Hebrew at New York's General Theological Seminary, wrote the poem as a Christmas gift to his children in 1822. Although Moore first published it (anonymously) in 1823 in the *Troy Sentinel* (New York) newspaper, he did not acknowledge himself as author until 1837. And it wasn't until 1844 that he included "A Visit from St. Nicholas" (the poem's actual title) in one of his own anthologies, coinciding with its wide acceptance as a

Folk-art toys help warm the pages of dePaola's version of *The Night Before Christmas.*

As the children "were nestled all snug in their beds," quilts, modeled after those in dePaola's personal collection, grace the pages of *The Night Before Christmas.*

beloved Christmas tradition. In choosing the 1840s for his setting, dePaola parallels the time when readers were becoming universally aware of the poem's existence.

While researching the ballad, dePaola discovered that Moore was undoubtedly influenced by Washington Irving's *Diedrich Knickerbocker's History of New York from the Beginning of the World to the End of the Dutch Dynasty,* in which the famous American storyteller makes reference to St. Nick.[2] Not only did Moore follow Irving's penchant to depict St. Nick as a sturdy pipe-smoking Dutchman, but his use of phrases such as "chubby and plump" and "laying his finger aside of his nose" also was probably influenced by Irving's text. Some 158 years later, dePaola followed Moore's lead, visually creating a pudgy, twinkly-eyed St. Nicholas that is a "right jolly old elf," and fashioning diminutive figures to suggest "a miniature sleigh with eight tiny reindeer."

Using the small New Hampshire town of Wilmot Flat, where dePaola lived at the time, as background, and his own house in particular, the artist imbues a New England rural flavor that sets this version apart from the many "anywhere" renditions available. He extends the ambience by wrapping his presentation in quilt designs, many of which are from his own New England quilt collection. This motif is carried out prudently: Multicolored square and diamond quilt-pattern borders frame the front of the jacket and the inside pages, a laid-out quilt decorates the back dust jacket, and the family members sleep "snug in their beds" under cheerily colored quilts within the story. While line rather than color is generally thought to be the means of energizing a story, here it is the dense hues that set each spread aglow and encourage the ever-important turn of the page. In executing the illustrations, dePaola says, "I chose colored inks on coarse paper so that the transparencies, used in the printing process at that time, would pick up the texture."

The outdoor scenes depict a Wilmot Flat that hasn't changed much in the last hundred or so years, complete with a war memorial statue, the local Baptist church, and clapboard houses, and the interior scenes are authentic to the time period. A plaid-covered wing chair stands near the fireplace, flowery stencils embellish a wall, woven rugs brighten wooden floors, and candles and kerosene lamps look ready for use. And, ever cognizant of the child reader, the artist punctuates the pages with early-nineteenth-century toys—wooden soldiers, striped balls, spinning tops, pull toys, hobby horses, soft dolls, and candy canes. When the book was published, dePaola held a celebration for Wilmot Flat residents in the town hall—a sign of his generosity and delight in Christmas festivities.

Inspiration for dePaola's opening title-page illustration in *The Night Before Christmas*, FAR RIGHT, derived from his then home, a nineteenth-century farmhouse in Wilmot Flat, New Hampshire, RIGHT.

DePaola's rendition is reminiscent of Grandma Moses's 1948 version.[3] Both are executed in a folkloric style that evokes the spirit of New England. Her small-village setting, while not as town-specific as dePaola's, also features quilt-covered beds; colorful woven rugs; hand-hewn furniture; and old-fashioned drums, horns, and other toys. Viewed simultaneously, the two provide an inviting exercise in contrast and comparison.

Another book—and one dePaola authored—that offers an interesting connection is *An Early American Christmas*. This story is also set, though somewhat earlier, in 1800s New Hampshire. It features a blond-haired, angular father whose physical proportions could put him in line as an ancestor to the father in dePaola's *The Night Before Christmas*. Having moved from Wilmot Flat to nearby New London by the time *An Early American Christmas* was published, dePaola used a generic setting for this historical-fiction picture book.

"And the neighbors came quietly to look, and to hear the Christmas songs coming from the house of 'the Christmas Family.'"
*An Early American Christmas*

An array of hands, shown from above, conveys the family's busy preparations for the Christmas holiday.
*An Early American Christmas*

The story tells of a family of German immigrants who settle in New England, bringing with them their many Christmas traditions. Throughout the busy year they find time to get ready for the holiday: dipping candles, storing the best apples, whittling a new character for the manger scene, creating paper tree decorations, baking cookies, and choosing a tree in the forest. On Christmas Eve, as candles shine from each window in the house and the sound of carols drifts over the countryside, their neighbors come to see and listen; next year, they, too, will enfold these beautiful traditions into their lives—traditions that will, of course, become part of the holiday across America and around the world.

In presenting his part-historical, part-fictional tale, dePaola expands on his signature folkloric style, creating some mesmerizing spreads. Immediately noticeable is the vast amount of white space. His soft-hued palette, shaded for texture, aptly reflects the colors of the time. By also incorporating a lot of white within the pictures, the artist injects the wintry atmosphere he wants. This technique results in a far different kind of winter setting than found in *The Night Before Christmas,* which, except for the snow scenes, is rich with color. Although close in subject matter and time period, these two books are rendered in different, yet totally appropriate, ways.

DePaola effectively utilizes sequence illustration in *An Early American Christmas* as he depicts the various processes involved in the family's candlemaking efforts.

In *An Early American Christmas,* spare, well-composed, and nicely spaced artwork is thoughtfully balanced by decorative details (a stylized evergreen, floating stars and hearts, geometric designs, and an—almost—ever-present cat). Introduced on the jacket, these elements carry through without being intrusive and bring a cohesiveness to the pages. Even more effective is the framing of many of the images. The family's home and a horn-blowing angel appear as hanging pictures in the front matter, the rafters and floor of the house often set off action scenes, a window reveals a change of season, and a huge tabletop becomes the work space for busy hands cutting out decorations. Brushed with soft colors, these "frames" often are embellished with wispy diamonds, dots, stripes, or rectangular bands. The total effect is pleasing.

Written in 1987, the book encompasses the 1990s interest in immigration and traditions passed down through families. On the penultimate page, the text reads, "As the years went by, some of the neighbors put candles in their windows too. Then Christmas trees appeared in their parlors. They began to sing Christmas songs. One by one every household in the village became a Christmas family."

Reaching out to others is a theme that runs through several of dePaola's books, but it is character and story that dictate his approach. Even in his cache of folktales, where message is often the crux of a story, the artist-author sculpts robust characters that strengthen his tellings and artistic images.

# Writing Is Like Cooking
*by Tomie dePaola*

I like to cook at Christmas—or any time for that matter—and I believe that writing a good manuscript is like making a good stock. You start by throwing all your scraps (your ideas)—onion peel, potato peel, carrot peel, old bones, you name it—into a pan of water. As that heats up, scum begins rising to the surface. It is very important to scoop that scum off the top of the liquid and get rid of the impurities from all the stuff you've put in. As the scum rises you need to continue to skim it off, and that takes a long time. One must be very patient. After all the scum is gone, you bring the stock to a soft rolling boil so there is a little more activity. The longer you let that stock (the experiences) slowly simmer, the more the essential flavors can come out of the ingredients. Now, at this point, you taste the stock, boosting the flavor by adding some peppercorns, some salt, some spices, letting them simmer together. Then, with layers of cheesecloth, you strain the stock, throwing all the leftovers away.

The next step is to take the liquid and reduce it to make the flavors strong. You may begin with three gallons and end up with only a half gallon—the more you reduce, the stronger the flavors will be. But your stock still is not finished. You have to continue to be patient and let it slowly boil away. If you want that stock (your plot) to be crystal clear, then you beat an egg white and its shell into the cold stock, which means you have to take it off the stove and let it sit for a while.

Now, you heat the stock up again very slowly, removing the last of the impurities that the egg white has brought to the surface. Then, very carefully, dip a ladle into the stock, remove it spoonful by spoonful, and hold it up to the light. Now you have a beautiful, crystal-clear, full-flavored stock. And that is just the way writing works.

When creating a picture book, you need to get down to the basic essentials. Of course, this varies somewhat depending on the book. A board book is like a snack—there are just a few words and only six illustrations, but an elaborate book, such as *The Legend of the Poinsettia,* is like a banquet with its many courses.

"Under the ashes of the tipi fire one stick still glowed. She took it and quietly crept out into the night." *The Legend of the Bluebonnet*

# Folktales

Folktales are a lifeline to the "humanness" of us all—our foibles, dreams, hurts, and joys—and dePaola's interest in these old stories parallels his interest in people: all kinds of people, all kinds of stories. A longtime reader and researcher of folktales, dePaola has not limited his repertoire, as many illustrators do, to the usual roster of Grimm, Perrault, and Andersen. His penchant runs to folktales rooted in his Italian and Irish heritage and to lesser-known stories from the U.S. and abroad. Many reflect his humor, some are filled with poignancy; all breathe with the exuberance the illustrator finds in life.

Before beginning the writing or artwork, dePaola does extensive research, looking for the "root tale" and reading every version he can find. Locating sources for *The Legend of Old Befana* found him on the floor of the Library of Congress, surrounded by dozens of titles. As with his other books, ideas for his retellings come sometimes from his family, sometimes from educators he meets on speaking and autographing tours, sometimes from collaborators, and sometimes from unexpected places. *Days of the Blackbird,* one of the illustrator's strongest offerings at this writing, is a case in point. One cold January night several years ago, dePaola tells, he ventured out to a restaurant near his home for dinner. His grumbles about the below-zero temperature prompted chef Piero Canuto[1] to say that in his home, the northern mountains of Italy, the bitter cold days of January are called *le giornate della merla* (the days of

77

the blackbird). The story goes, he says, that once-white doves turned soot black—a color they have remained to this day—when wintry weather forced them to hide in chimney tops to stay warm. Intrigued by this fragment of a legend, dePaola set off on a research trail that resulted in *Days of the Blackbird,* a book compelling for its narrative and visual

Just as her father had promised, the snows would melt, the trees would sprout buds, and then one day, the clear song of La Colomba would fly through the windows and into the Great Hall. She was always the first to return. In no time at all, the courtyard was filled with flowers and birds. Duca Gennaro and Gemma would take their places under the trees and listen to the beautiful melodies.

authenticity. While the artist says that he might have used a lighter mode of approach, he decided to tip the story toward an Emperor's Nightingale-type of tale; a wise choice, as it allowed him to use a painterly style for his illustrations, lending a quiet elegance, and to draw on his love of Italian frescoes.

In *Days of the Blackbird*, dePaola captures the essence of the passing seasons through strong use of color; thoughtful placement of La Columba guides the eye surely across the double-page spread.

In a salute to his key source, dePaola roots the story in Sabbia, the chef's childhood home. A double-page-spread title page depicts mountains soaring above the village, and as the book progresses, occasional glimpses of the peaks appear through the high windows and arched doorways of Duca Gennaro's opulent home, the story's main setting. A large full-color photograph of the scene, which hangs on the restaurant's wall, provided the inspiration and graphic authority. Each afternoon, Gemma (which means "jewel" in Italian) and her father, Duca Gennaro (the Italian word for January), enjoy the sweet songs of the many birds that live in their tree-filled courtyard. One, a pure white dove that Gemma calls La Colomba, has the clearest melody of all.

When the duke becomes ill, Gemma begs the birds not to fly south as it gets colder, but one by one they leave. Only La Colomba stays the winter, after Gemma convinces her that her singing is what is keeping her father alive. But during the last frozen days of January, the cold becomes so intense that the bird takes to sleeping in a nearby chimney top. When she emerges, the soot has turned her into *la merla*, the blackbird, which she is still called today. And so, by enlarging the fragment into a full narrative thread and peopling it with intriguing characters and events, dePaola suggests how that old legend might have begun.

Not far from the Piedmont area, the setting for *Days of the Blackbird*, are the Dolomites. A story from this part of Italy, which was brought to dePaola's attention by then fellow teacher Linda Morley,[2] resulted in the magical moon story *The Prince of the Dolomites.* In this tale, dePaola relates how the once-dark Dolomite mountains were changed to glimmering peaks of white, blue, and yellow. By using a story-within-a-story technique, the author not only provides background for the somewhat complex tale, but ties in, at the close, a minitale of how edelweiss—*stella alpina*—came to bloom on the mountaintops of Italy. Here dePaola's style is more formal than usual and his illustrations—well-spaced images balanced with small decorative designs—follow in the same tradition. The transformation of the mountains, which is at the heart of the plot, involves a band of tiny people called the Salvani, "protectors of all that is nature." These are not tricksters in the leprechaun/troll tradition of Irish and Scandinavian lore but a kindhearted lot, whose appearances on two strategic occasions turn the action.

Important to the child reader, and hence to dePaola, is what happens in a story; action, in fact, is what charges most of his tales. As in any good literary piece, action must be linked to a strong, believable character who carries the events forward; someone to root for during the climax and cheer for at the conclusion. This necessary element is not lost on dePaola the author or dePaola the artist. A study of his retellings evinces that he leans to tales where already-strong characters can be fashioned into even more dynamic portrayals through stringent word choice and fine wielding of the paintbrush.

This is clearly seen in *Days of the Blackbird,* where his depiction of Gemma as an intrepid and determined protagonist is reflected in both text and image. Another example is Lore, a medieval gatekeeper's daughter, whose courage Patricia Lee Gauch and dePaola celebrated in *Once Upon a Dinkelsbühl.* A painting on the town hall in that small Bavarian village visualizes Lore confronting the colonel of the invading army, asking for a reprieve for her townsfolk.[3] The children of Dinkelsbühl reenact the story each summer, drawing people from around the world.

Another legendary character, this time a Native American, that dePaola has brought vividly to life is She-Who-Is-Alone. DePaola learned of this legend through Texas reading consultant Margaret Looper,[4] who initially supplied him with the basics about the bluebonnet tale featured in *The Legend of the Bluebonnet* and who continued to be helpful through the writing and illustrative processes. In that story, a young girl bravely sacrifices her beloved doll to the flames to save her people.

By contrasting the deep blues of the sky with the swirling reddish orange hues of the fire, dePaola electrifies this heart-wrenching scene from *The Legend of the Bluebonnet.*

As the story begins, the people call to the Great Spirits to heal their sun-parched land. She-Who-Is-Alone, who has already lost her parents and grandparents to the famine, listens nearby, clasping her beloved warrior doll. When the shaman brings word that rain will come only with the sacrifice of a "most valued possession," She-Who-Is-Alone vows silently to give up her doll. At night, she climbs alone to a hilltop, where she flings this most prized possession into the fire. As she does so, her soulful eyes, the brave tilt of her chin, and the determined hunch to her shoulders form a compelling visual image. For dramatic impact, dePaola isolates her on the page.

In keeping with the Texas setting, the artist gives this Comanche tale an open and free-flowing appearance. At the beginning, he crowds together rounded-backed, bowed-head characters against a stark landscape at page bottom, and further expands the mood with earth-toned clothing and solemn expressions. Then, as She-Who-Is-Alone undertakes her solitary mission, the night sky darkens and fills with stars, the red-and-gold flame spirals into a cobalt blue sky, and the winds scatter the ashes across the heavens. After the morning rain, the fallen ashes cover the hills with blue flowers—a sign of forgiveness from the Great Spirits.

Drama and emotion emerge through body posture rather than facial expression in these two scenes from *The Legend of the Bluebonnet*, RIGHT, and from *The Legend of the Indian Paintbrush*, FAR RIGHT.

Now called bluebonnet, this Texas state flower blankets the country-side each spring. Here, dePaola brings white space back into play, using it to elicit a feeling of distance. He also introduces a rich palette of greens, yellows, and blues, which balances the presentation and brings deft closure to the tale.

Changes of mood and emotion through color also appear in *The Legend of the Indian Paintbrush*, a Plains Indian folktale. The idea for this book about Wyoming's state flower grew from a conversation dePaola had with Pat Henry, a Wyoming educator.[5] While researching the paint-brush legend, dePaola found the existing stories too adult-oriented, so he removed much of the bloodshed and introduced a child into his retelling. Although Little Gopher lacks the physical prowess of the other boys, his Dream-Vision reveals that he will one day be a great painter. Eventually, he brings the colors of the sunset down to earth and his paintbrushes flower into the brilliant colors that now sweep the western plains each summer. The legend seems a natural choice for dePaola to illustrate, for it contains the same themes close to his heart and ones found in his other books: love of painting (*The Art Lesson*), ostracism of peers (*Oliver Button Is a Sissy*), and following one's own vision (*The Clown of God*).

Not only has dePaola cramped a muddled Fin into a cradle, but he escalates the farce by contrasting the giant with the tiny creatures that hover just out of his sight. *Fin M'Coul, the Giant of Knockmany Hill*

Not all dePaola's choices for folktale retellings are of a serious nature. For instance, the Irish hero Fin M'Coul has rarely been realized in more side-splitting humor than he is in *Fin M'Coul, the Giant of Knockmany Hill.* Funny indeed is the scene where, in an attempt to fool the nasty Cucullin, a baby-clothed Fin rocks away in a cradle. But there is more to making humor than just the costuming: Strategic use of space and size is at the center of this comedy.

Because the text is placed at the bottoms of the pages in this over-size book, dePaola has just the top two-thirds for illustration—a clever and highly workable device for this particular story. An unadorned brown border edged in pink restricts the pictorial space further, so that Fin, his wife Oonagh, and Cucullin appear as the ample giants they are. To accentuate their size, the artist crops their heads at the crown—or, in the case of the mean Cucullin, just above his close-spaced, beady eyes—and at times bleeds the pictures to the border. This kind of deliberate crowding not only enhances the appearance of size but also punctuates the story's inherent buffoonery. In further playful positioning, small leprechauns and fairies dance at the giants' feet and scuttle around the edges of the pages.

Considering dePaola's impish nature, it seems natural to find such tiny fantastical characters tucked into many of his books. Their presence often adds to the appeal and gives an artistic symmetry to the story. Decorative in *Fin M'Coul,* the creatures can play a dominant role. The pukwudgies (American Indian) in Jean Fritz's *The Good Giants and the Bad Pukwudgies* and the tengu (Japanese) in Tony Johnston's *The Badger and the Magic Fan* are mischief-makers of the first degree; a leprechaun (Irish) sets the events in motion in *Jamie O'Rourke and the Big Potato;* trolls (Norwegian) are the ones outwitted in *The Cat on the Dovrefell;* and in *Helga's Dowry,* the troll Helga determines the action.

Calling on his love of film technique here to embellish humor, dePaola comically depicts the villagers' growing distaste for eating potatoes in *Jamie O'Rourke and the Big Potato.*

85

DePaola's own delight in mischief blooms fully in his illustrations for Tony Johnston's *The Tale of Rabbit and Coyote,* a *pourquoi* story about why coyotes howl at the moon. Detractors of dePaola's work who remark on the similarity of his illustrations should look carefully here. Continuing in his folkloric style, the illustrator gives this Oaxacan tale a Mexican flavor. Colors resound with spicy, sun-hot tones, and stylized shapes echo designs of primitive folk objects.

Climbing a ladder to the moon, which deftly exhibits Rabbit's silliness in *The Tale of Rabbit and Coyote,* results in a much different reaction—a highly poignant moment—in another dePaola book, *Sing, Pierrot, Sing,* on page 108.

The illustrator's facile manipulation of shape surfaces in several whimsical and distinctive ways. On intensely colored single-page spreads, border-decorated squares provide the stage, undulating hills, stylized cacti, and spare-leaved trees the background. Coyote and Rabbit, who race across the pages in silly attempts to outdo each other, are smoothly contoured in bright teal and purple. Spanish words, worked into the pictures, often imitate the forms of other objects on the page. All these elements fuse together, emphasizing the nonsense while anchoring the tale to its place of origin. In *Erandi's Braids,* dePaola's palette again showcases the colors of the Southwest. Here, however, the artist uses the vibrant hues as background and evocative characterizations to carry forth Antonio Hernández Madrigal's self-sacrifice theme—in a story that has touchstones in dePaola's own *The Legend of the Bluebonnet.*

Another offering from Johnston, an ofttime dePaola collaborator, is *Alice Nizzy Nazzy: The Witch of Santa Fe,* a Baba Yaga variant that also

As in *The Legend of the Bluebonnet*, dePaola shows that expression need not always come through the face; in *Erandi's Braids*, the women's braids tell a story of their own.

carries elements, if one looks, from Hansel and Gretel. Johnston, who loves the Russian Baba Yaga stories, wanted a new landscape for the familiar tale. In this story, she pits a young shepherd girl, Manuela, against the nasty Alice Nizzy Nazzy. When her sheep are stolen, Manuela immediately heads for the adobe roadrunner house of Alice Nizzy Nazzy to get them back. Although the witch puts Manuela in a cooking pot and threatens to eat her, the young protagonist eventually outwits the conniving hag.

The tale allowed dePaola to delve again into his love of the Southwest, reflected in the bright, rich colors and use of Mexican-influenced motifs. Johnston did the same, using an adobe roadrunner house instead of a traditional chicken-footed one and including a Southwest native horned lizard as Alice Nizzy Nazzy's pet.

While Rabbit and Coyote's battle calls for a more tightly controlled design, in *Alice Nizzy Nazzy*, dePaola lets his artwork spill to the page borders, with only a bright, narrow coral border to center the action. Always cognizant of balance and harmony, dePaola fashions an outrageous Alice Nizzy Nazzy, whose yellow face, green chile hair, and orange-and-black teeth reek of evildoing. Manuela, on the other hand, is more complex. Her round eyes and stand-out-straight braids express an initial naïveté, and her lace-collared, aproned dress belies, at first, her feisty

87

The vibrant colors of Alice Nizzy Nazzy's headband, earrings, and fingernails, echoed in Manuela's dress and in two flashes of fire, provide balance and visual stimulation in *Alice Nizzy Nazzy*.

and stalwart nature. She is, however, as readers discover, quite equal to the task of retrieving her stolen sheep.

In an afterword to the book, dePaola refers to the possibility of Alice Nizzy Nazzy and Strega Nona being "close cousins." Both are witches, and both have the ability to shrink and expand their houses when needed, but there, the artist assures readers, the resemblance ends. (This is the reason, dePaola says, somewhat tongue in cheek, why Strega Nona's house changes its size!) For many readers, "dear Strega Nona," as dePaola calls her, has slipped into the realm of folklore. Some claim to have heard tales of her at their mothers' proverbial knees, while a Chicago entrepreneur named his restaurant Strega Nona, contending that the figure is so familiar that it is in the public domain. Never mind that one day, many years ago, during a faculty meeting, Strega Nona appeared, according to the artist, unannounced and unsolicited while he was doodling on his drawing pad.[6]

Both Alice Nizzy Nazzy and Strega Nona's houses have "magical qualities," claims dePaola, and, he hopes, young readers will "enjoy their possibilities on and off the page."

"Nothing much happened in the little town in Calabria where
Strega Nona lived." *Strega Nona Meets Her Match*

# Strega Nona

From a bulbous-nosed, protruding-chinned face on that doodling pad, Strega Nona has emerged as a highly familiar figure in children's literature. Not satisfied to be the heroine of five books—*Strega Nona, Big Anthony and the Magic Ring, Strega Nona's Magic Lessons, Merry Christmas, Strega Nona,* and *Strega Nona Meets Her Match*—she then revealed "all" in a biography, *Strega Nona, Her Story,* as told to Tomie dePaola. (Not to be left behind, in 1998, Big Anthony claimed his own top billing in *Big Anthony, His Story.*) The star of several successful dramatizations by the Children's Theatre Company of Minneapolis,[1] Strega Nona has been replicated as a soft cloth doll; appears on wall hangings, T-shirts, Christmas ornaments, needlepoint pillows, mugs, and tote bags; graced the World Financial Center at Rizzoli's Book Fair; provided a huge background presence during dePaola's presentation at Universal Studios in Orlando as a gigantic balloon; and turns up in background detail in a number of dePaola's books. Strega Nona has, indeed, come a long way.[2]

So what makes this grandma witch so enduring? Possibly it's the folkloric quality of the tales, or the combination of silliness and warm-hearted truthfulness embedded in the plots, or the ever-child-appealing directness of delivery, or even the Italian aura of sun-warmed colors and brisk lines that enliven the action. More likely it's a blend of

Strega Nona works magic over
her pasta pot. *Strega Nona*

these ingredients, and the integrated way in which the artist-author presents them.

After Strega Nona's introduction, when an astute Caldecott committee saluted her arrival with a silver Honor Book designation in 1976,[3] three years passed before each of her next two appearances (1979 and 1982), four years before the next (1986), and then a seven-year and another three-year gap (1993, 1996) before the author took up her story again. According to dePaola, another book in the series, tentatively titled *Strega Nona Goes on Vacation,* will appear early in the new century. Although dePaola worked on a number of other titles in the intervening years, the vigor he bestows on these characters maintains the tales' continuity.

Readers meet Strega Nona in a small village in Calabria, a southern Italian province—and dePaola's ancestral home. There she busily administers potions, cures, comfort, and advice, carefully portioned with bits of magic—and love. Her pasta pot, for instance, needs three kisses to make it stop boiling—a lesson her bumbling hired helper Big Anthony learns the hard way in *Strega Nona.* DePaola reveals the secret ingredient of her magic in *Strega Nona, Her Story* when Grandma Concetta[4] passes on the spell to her young granddaughter (who becomes Strega Nona), reminding her that "you must blow three kisses and the pot will stop. For that is the *ingrediente segreto*—LOVE. It is the same with all your magic. Always Love." It is, of course, dePaola's underlying message to young readers—that love should underscore their work and their lives.

The love ingredient is certainly central to dePaola's work. One sees it in his own interactions with children in library or classroom settings and in the way he involves them in his books. He treats his characters thoughtfully, infuses them with dignity, and injects a warmth that radiates off the page. In putting children at the center in what he writes and illustrates, dePaola creates a direct line to their hearts and to their intellects. As Bette Peltola, Chair of the 1990 United States Hans Christian Andersen Committee, wrote in presenting dePaola as the U.S. nominee for the International Board on Books for Young People's Illustrator Award, "His illustrations capture and reflect the mood of the text and always are clear in meaning to the child reader."[5] Children relate, for example, to how the brusque but kindhearted Strega Nona takes in the awkward Big Anthony, the overworked Bambolona, and the scheming Strega Amelia, and to how she continues to get Big Anthony out of scrapes, sends Bambolona back to her father to help out when times are tight, and wishes her rival, Strega Amelia, the best.

The disparity of the flamboyantly dressed Strega Amelia and the homespun-outfitted Strega Nona adds life to the characters and humor to the story. *Strega Nona Meets Her Match*

In dePaola's autobiographical stories, the characters of Tommy and others may play out incidents from the artist-author's childhood, but the heart of dePaola the adult lodges in Strega Nona. While she mixes magic into her spells, dePaola dispenses magic in another way. In the guise of this toothless, somewhat bossy old woman, he disseminates messages about being happy with oneself, the need for generosity, and the importance of love. "Children," dePaola says, "are the hope of our future, and we must treat them as such. This may sound trite, but it's true."

Subtle though they are, his messages are ones that children won't miss. Sending a message, however, is definitely not on dePaola's agenda when writing and illustrating: "Books are a fantasy-oriented way to learn basic truths. Truths, not morals. I avoid moralizing at all costs."

Strega Nona herself would be the last person to burden her friends with moral messages; she is far too busy enjoying life—and keeping Big Anthony out of trouble. The first of the Strega Nona books, a "sorcerer's apprentice/magic porridge pot" sort of tale, finds Big Anthony, whom Strega Nona hires as a handyman, foolishly starting Strega Nona's magic pasta pot boiling when she is away, without knowing how to stop it. He nearly floods the town with pasta before Strega Nona returns and rescues the situation.

"[Strega Nona] didn't have to look twice to know
what had happened." *Strega Nona*

In *Big Anthony and the Magic Ring,* Big Anthony continues his bumbling quest to learn Strega Nona's magic spells. After seeing how she transformed herself into a beautiful young lady for an evening of dancing the tarantella, Big Anthony decides to use the ring for a night of fun for himself. As a handsome cavalier, he dances away the evening in the company of a coterie of adoring ladies. Soon, however, their ceaseless attentions overwhelm him, and again Strega Nona must extricate him from a spell. But does he learn his lesson? Not Big Anthony.

By placing a tall, gallant Big Anthony amid a bevy of love-struck ladies, dePaola smoothly effects a character change in Strega Nona's inept helper. *Big Anthony and the Magic Ring*

He is determined to learn magic, and when Strega Nona takes on Bambolona as her protégée in *Strega Nona's Magic Lessons,* a jealous Big Anthony disguises himself as Antonia, even though the breadmaker's wife rebukes him with "Whoever heard of a man being a Strega?" However, the canny Strega Nona is not one who is easily fooled, and she tricks Big Anthony into thinking he has turned her into a frog. DePaola coordinates text and image well. Only through Bambolona's sly smirks and Strega Nona's craggy face watching Big Anthony wailing at the sight of the frog do readers know that Strega Nona has thoroughly bamboozled her helper. Big Anthony vows, "I'll never play with magic again." But one wonders!

All the scene's key ingredients—a scolding Bambolona, a contrite Big Anthony, a sly Strega Nona, and an innocent frog—are cleverly yet simply integrated into one cohesive image. *Strega Nona's Magic Lessons*

Narrative and image must work hand in hand, extending each other. This kind of visual synergy—so evident in the Strega Nona stories—is what makes dePaola such a master of the picture-book form. Not only is every page well designed, with careful attention to gutters and margins and the constrictions of the page, but dePaola is aware of the flow between story and picture and from page to page. These natural limitations of a picture book, ignored by too many illustrators, are built-in considerations for this artist.

From time to time, small design inconsistencies do creep in—sometimes a bare tree stands beside Strega Nona's house, at other times it's a cypress, and at still other times it's a stylized design; and a small nearby goat shed appears and disappears without explanation. "It's part of Strega Nona's magic," dePaola claims with a twinkle in his eye, and who can argue with that?

While children do benefit from the artist's compositional skills, they are more appreciative of the visual extras that appear throughout many of his books. In *Merry Christmas, Strega Nona,* angels peer in Strega Nona's windows, hover over the manger, and smile from rooftops, while

singing emanates from red-cloaked shepherds (Could one be Charlie? The protagonist of *"Charlie Needs a Cloak"* is a frequent background visitor in dePaola's books). He also implants references from past Strega Nona titles (her hillside house, her animals, her friend Strega Amelia) while allowing the story to stand on its own. In another nod to the visual extras children enjoy as well as to dePaola's own playful nature, the newly acclaimed "author" of *Strega Nona, Her Story* poses for her portrait on the back dust jacket flap, and on the back cover entertains the townspeople at a book signing. As *Strega Nona, Her Story* ends, dePaola brings the legend full circle by repeating an incident found in the first title. Strega Nona posts a wanted sign in the village square for a helper and then finds, on the last page, the gawky Big Anthony at her door. And, as the text reads, "The rest is history."

Big Anthony, too, enjoys a book signing following his debut as "author." In introducing *Big Anthony, His Story,* dePaola gives readers his slyest visual joke to date. On the dust jacket, the familiar blond-haired bumbler, serenely framed, appears in a Mona Lisa pose.[6] And could those be Monet's haystacks decorating the background? From there, the artist-author takes readers back in time to the birth of Big Anthony, amusing them with hilarious episodes from his early life, and finally delivering them to the little house on the hill in Calabria where he knocks on the door and finds himself face to face with Strega Nona. Once again, we read the words "The rest is history." And once again, dePaola's agile story-making causes us to smile.

"The rest is history." While the same text concludes the tales, the illustrations give two different perspectives as readers look in and out of the doorway of Strega Nona's house. *Strega Nona, Her Story* and *Big Anthony, His Story*

"Mary had a little lamb / Its fleece was white as snow / And everywhere that Mary went / The lamb was sure to go." *Mary Had a Little Lamb*

# Story Making

The desire to write stories, as well as to illustrate them, was always part of dePaola's career plans. His first attempt—and second publishing effort—was a (short-lived) original tale, *The Wonderful Dragon of Timlin*; he followed it with a quartet of stories—*Fight the Night, Joe and the Snow, Parker Pig, Esquire,* and *The Monsters' Ball*—which, he says, "are best counted as learning experiences." Most of his energy during these early publishing years was concentrated on sharpening his illustrator techniques, but gradually tales of his own began taking shape in his mind.

*When Everyone Was Fast Asleep,* for instance, is a poetic tale derived from a time when dePaola was living in California and became interested in dream therapy. The story features Token, the Fog Maiden's sloe-eyed cat, who leads two small children into the enchanted world of night, where they meet an elf horse, eat honey with trolls, and watch a theatrical performance with a king and queen. The pencil-shaded, gauzy-looking illustrations provide an ethereal look, and a larger-than-life Token brings cohesion to the somewhat slight story. Beyond that, the book merits notice as dePaola's first touch with poetry and, from the illustrative side, for the way images from his books—past and future—weave in and out of the pictures in much the same way mirages float through dreams.

During their journey, the two children see a Strega Nona look-alike (*Strega Nona* had been published the year before), trolls right out of *Helga's Dowry* (released the same year), and an alligator and a commedia

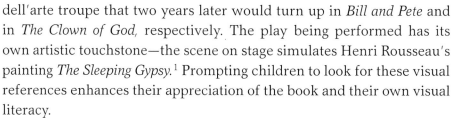

dell'arte troupe that two years later would turn up in *Bill and Pete* and in *The Clown of God,* respectively. The play being performed has its own artistic touchstone—the scene on stage simulates Henri Rousseau's painting *The Sleeping Gypsy.*[1] Prompting children to look for these visual references enhances their appreciation of the book and their own visual literacy.

Interpreting the masters is a graphic technique dePaola enjoys using and one he ingeniously takes advantage of in *Bonjour, Mr. Satie.* Part of the story takes place in a Paris salon of the 1920s, where dePaola inserts a guitar-playing cat in the "blue period" style of Picasso's *The Old Guitarist.*[2] This witty depiction is especially fitting, since the main character, Mr. Satie the cat, is an art critic.

In 1989, when dePaola wrote and illustrated *The Art Lesson,* his thrust was to show a young boy's confrontation with his art teacher and to provide, through his own childhood experience, a peek into children's beginning creativity. Two years later, in *Bonjour, Mr. Satie,* the illustrator offered a more sophisticated look at the other end of artistic endeavor—accomplished artists who have already proven their worth. Both books

delve into the deep feelings people have about art, the need for individual expression, and the pleasure found in drawing and painting. With these two books, dePaola has created a circle, as he has with the Strega Nona books. And because *Bonjour, Mr. Satie* is told as a story-within-a-story, a favorite device of dePaola's, this book becomes a circle in itself. It is also another example of dePaola's leading the way: Since the publication of *Bonjour, Mr. Satie,* several other authors have put allusions to famous adults in their books.[3]

Recently returned from Paris, Uncle Satie amuses his niece and nephew, Rosalie and Conrad, with one of his adventures in the French capital. This episode relates how Uncle Satie successfully mediates an argument that breaks out at his friend Gertrude's Sunday evening salon attended by various luminaries of the Parisian art scene. The quarrel between Henri and Pablo centers on whose paintings are the best, but soon everyone enters the fray.[4] After careful scrutiny, Mr. Satie declares (in a splendid piece of wordplay by dePaola) that "the contest is a draw."

From start to finish, the book is handsomely presented, and its theme—that art is a matter of taste—is delivered with wit and aplomb. It is a

A sweep of emotions dominates the page as dePaola incorporates facial expression and hand positioning to visualize the action. A thrust-out arm nicely accommodates the inner margin and brings cohesion to the picture. *Bonjour, Mr. Satie*

Pablo put his paintings against one wall.
Henri put his paintings against the other.
Everyone started talking at once, taking sides.
"Pablo is brilliant! Henri is boring!" shouted one group.
"Henri is a genius! Pablo is weird!" shouted the other group.

theme that needs to be reinforced with children, who often doubt their own artistic abilities.

The jacket sets the scene: Mr. Satie, a debonair-looking cat, and his companion, Ffortusque Ffollet Esq., a bespectacled, knickers-clad mouse, are seen strolling the Champs-Élysées; the Eiffel Tower and the Arc de Triomphe stand in the background. The book's front matter includes a postcard to Rosalie and Conrad informing them of Uncle Satie's arrival, and a two-page spread, which doubles as the title page, depicting Mr. Satie and Fortie as they journey by steamship, train, and taxi to Rosalie and Conrad's home in America.

In these opening scenes, the use of animals as characters lends a playful note, a touch the artist extends through white backgrounds and pastel colors. During the flashback, the white space is eliminated; the text is placed in red-bordered, gray-mottled boxes; colors become deeper and richer; and the characters, with the exception of Mr. Satie and Fortie, all are human. At the close, dePaola reverts to his opening style, crisply setting off the story-within-a-story sequence.

"Oh, oh, oh," cried Alice.
"A duel!" the Russian prince shouted.
"A prizefight!" yelled the American writer.
"Call the gendarme!" screamed Pablo's wife.
"Enough, enough, enough," bellowed Gertrude.
And they all stopped at once.

Both indoor and outdoor episodes in Paris are imbued with the city's famous charm—café-lined streets, flowerpot-decorated windowsills, red chimney-topped houses, and galleries overflowing with paintings. The characters are aptly portrayed, and while children may not readily recognize such names as Pablo, Henri, Gertrude, and Alice, that's not important. Some youngsters will find their curiosities satisfied by perceptive teachers and other adults; others may remember, years later, a book carrying these names and make the connection; still others will just enjoy the tale. And when the battle royal breaks out as to whose pictures are the best (Pablo's or Henri's), children will identify with the crisis. The book also provides an opportunity for discussion concerning people's taste in art. In Mr. Satie's words: "I have concluded that to compare Henri's paintings of Nice with Pablo's paintings of newspapers, guitars, and faces from all different sides would be to compare apples with oranges. Both are delicious but taste totally different."

For the older reader, the book can be an insightful introduction to some of the real people in the story, who are partially identified on the back flap with first names and last initials (Claude M., Josephine B., Isadora D., Zelda F., Ernest H., etc.).[5] It also can provide a wider understanding of the early twentieth-century Parisian scene and of the relationships among and even beyond these figures. For example, Picasso was a close friend of the artist Georges Braque, who, although not included in the book, painted *Still Life with Score by Satie*[6] in honor of his friend and composer Erik Satie, whose name dePaola gave his real-life Abyssinian cat.[7]

DePaola's penchant for using windows to spotlight characters emerges, ABOVE, as Pierrot dreams of his beloved Columbine and, RIGHT, as Harlequin and Columbine toss away the clown's offered rose. *Sing, Pierrot, Sing*

Color plays an important role in the illustrations in *Bonjour, Mr. Satie*; but when a book has no text, such as *Sing, Pierrot, Sing: A Picture Book in Mime,* the way color is applied is even more crucial—and sometimes a bit risky. DePaola takes that risk, successfully, in *Pierrot*. After all, what could be more natural than telling a mime story without words? By incorporating the characters' traditional motifs—Pierrot's white-masked face and white pantalooned outfit, Harlequin's blue-and-gray diamond-patterned tunic, and Columbine's pink skirt and flower-garlanded headdress—into the art, dePaola forms the characters' identities. He also gives the story continuity by using a vibrant blue sky and milky sliver of a moon as background throughout, except for the opening sequence, which helps orient viewers as this tale of unrequited love unfolds.

As in many of his books, dePaola's fondness for the theater is evident: Backdrops resemble stage sets; the action, which takes place front and center, is seen from one perspective; and his penchant for introducing characters by placing them in windows brings attention to them as a spotlight does on the stage. Readers first see Pierrot sitting in a window, dreaming of his beloved Columbine, who is visualized in a balloon over his head. In subsequent pictures, Columbine—again framed, this time by a Juliet-like balcony—appears in Pierrot's daydreams. Readers meet Harlequin, having a tête-à-tête with his beloved Columbine off to the side, while the unsuspecting Pierrot, again in a window, pens a song to her.

The traditional story is given a child-centered twist. When the lovesick clown, rose and mandolin in hand, comes to serenade Columbine, a crowd of villagers gathers. In the scene where Harlequin tosses away the rose

Pierrot's anguish, the lovers' nonchalance, the villagers' heartless laughter, and the children's compassion all are reflected in one harmonious image.

The ladder and moon motif is used poignantly in *Sing, Pierrot, Sing.*

meant for Columbine, dePaola creates an ingenious juxtaposition of human reaction: While the watching adults laugh at Pierrot's distress, the children look on with concern and sympathy.

After learning that Columbine's heart belongs to Harlequin, Pierrot climbs to the moon in despair. The children, who find the unwanted rose and discarded mandolin, seek out the clown and offer a gift of love and music. He climbs down the ladder and, rejuvenated, joins them in singing and dancing under the moon.

Color also plays a part in dePaola's turn-of-the-century story *Marianna May and Nursey.* Young Marianna May loves to roll in the grass, make mud pies, eat strawberry ice cream, and paint pictures, but this poor little rich girl is always, just like Nursey, dressed completely in white. No matter that Marianna May's huge white hair bow, white high-necked, puffed-sleeved Edwardian dress, white stockings, and white button shoes inhibit her play. When her unhappy state comes to the attention of Mr.

Talbot, the iceman, he enlists the help of the kitchen staff, who, with several cartons of dye, change Marianna May's life. Soon Marianna May has a green dress for rolling in the grass, a brown dress for making mud pies, a pink dress for eating strawberry ice cream, and a rainbow-colored dress for painting pictures. And, oh yes, she still wears a white outfit—but only when playing in the snow.

DePaola's tongue-in-cheek emphasis on "whiteness" can be seen in the family portrait on the first page, in which Marianna May and her mother and father all are dressed in white; in the huge white dog that appears on nearly every page but is never mentioned in the text; in the white porch swing Marianna sits on to "keep [her] white dress clean"; and in the white backgrounds found throughout the book. For balance, dePaola nicely backs the family pose with rose-colored drapes, adds bright pink pillows to the swing, and brushes the dog's nose with pink. The Edwardian atmosphere perfectly fits the tale, which has its origins in a family photograph of dePaola's mother with a large bow in her hair. "An image," he says, "that took root and became a story."

A strong narrative thread, dePaola believes, is necessary—especially in a wordless book; it is an element he worked hard on in *Pancakes for Breakfast*, his first wordless endeavor. A country lady's attempts to make a breakfast of pancakes are hindered by a scarcity of ingredients and her pets' gluttonous hunger. While words do appear in a hand-lettered recipe, the pictures carry the story: A clock and a changing sky signal the passing hours, pictures in balloons show the woman's anticipation (a stack of pancakes dripping with butter), and facial expressions provide amusement. The use of a horizontal format enhances the simple, linear story line.

A horizontal format is employed also in dePaola's Bill and Pete stories, which now number three: *Bill and Pete, Bill and Pete Go Down the Nile,* and *Bill and Pete to the Rescue.* The droll escapades of Bill the crocodile and his friend, a bird named Pete, stretch out across the double-page spreads. The artist sustains visual interest with funny scenes of grinning white crocodile teeth and happy colors in sync with the unfolding melodrama. The hilarious malapropisms, Bill's fear that his missing father is now a suitcase, and visual clues to the mystery are deft touches, again evincing dePaola's versatility with pen and brush.

The opportunity to embellish and enlarge a text visually is one the artist feels strongly about. "Pictures can do the writing," dePaola asserts. "They do more than help the story; they amplify it. There must be room in the story line for the creation of images that invite the child's imagination to wander. The other world of things unsaid and unexplained

This child with a large white bow on her head, ABOVE, grew up and became dePaola's mother; the photograph inspired the story about a proper but bored Edwardian girl who is continually told to "sit nicely on the porch swing and keep your white dress clean," FAR LEFT. *Marianna May and Nursey*

is what I try to find, see, and portray." While in some ways, dePaola admits, writing his own stories gives him more freedom for visual play, working with another writer is a challenge he also finds exciting.

In the world of collaboration, dePaola has enjoyed the company of top writers in the field, such as Jean Fritz, Patricia MacLachlan, Jane Yolen, Steven Kroll, Nancy Willard, and Sarah Josepha Hale. Hale, of course, was a silent partner, having written "Mary Had a Little Lamb" in 1830. DePaola takes the classic poem beyond the familiar: He includes all six verses, rarely done, and weaves them into a full-blown imaginative and highly visual treatment. Beneath opening notes about the poem's background, he pictures Hale's home in Newport, New Hampshire, and on the title page portrays the woman at her writing desk, looking down at a lamb pull-toy as though it were providing the source of her inspiration. Music is included as well as the lyrics for all six verses.

Typical New England backgrounds and the homespun look of the costumes and other details befit the poem, and dePaola makes good use of space. One scene cleverly emphasizes the line "And everywhere that Mary went, the lamb was sure to go" by showing a sequential scene in a cutaway of the farmhouse. In another spread, he places the duo in a series of embracing circles: The bending tree bough, the shape of Mary's head and skirt, the position of Mary's arms, and the tilt of the lamb's head all lovingly accent the closeness of the two.

While dePaola has nimbly helped bring some of Jean Fritz's historical figures alive—in *Can't You Make Them Behave, King George?* and *The Great Adventure of Christopher Columbus: A Pop-up Book*—and has punched up the humor of Steven Kroll's *Fat Magic* and Daniel Pinkwater's *The Wuggie Norple Story*, the collaborator with whom he has most often shared the title page is Tony Johnston. The two have worked on nine books together, many of them folktale retellings but some of them original stories. DePaola calls Johnston a "dream to work with; she leaves huge textual gaps for me as illustrator to fill in."

In *The Quilt Story*, for example, a frontier mother stitches a quilt for her daughter, Abigail—one decorated with shooting stars and bordered

Pleasing symmetry is brought to the page through the oval picture of the long-ago Abigail, the circular designs in the quilt, and the roundness of the sleeping girl's face, the cat, and the doll's head. *The Quilt Story*

Rustic colors and patterns of stars come together in this image from *The Quilt Story.*

with red hearts and white doves. Abigail uses the quilt for a gown, as a tea party tablecloth, and to keep warm on the windswept prairie. When her family moves farther west, Abigail finds the quilt comforting amid all the newness of her new home. Eventually the quilt is put into the attic, where it lies forgotten until another young girl, generations later, finds the keepsake—badly in need of repair. Her mother patches the holes and puts in fresh padding, making the quilt whole and beautiful once again. And when this family relocates, the quilt provides the needed comfort to make the girl content in her new home.

Two poignant images give extra dimension to the story. When the second (and unnamed) girl discovers the old quilt, readers will see an oval picture of young Abigail and her cloth doll among the attic clutter. Then, in the penultimate image, the modern-day girl is seen in bed, snuggled under the quilt. At her side is the cloth doll, and above her bed hangs Abigail's portrait—connections across the ages. While providing a story that touches on pioneer days, relocation, family history, passing down family treasures, and, of course, quilts, Johnston and dePaola leave lots of room for children's imaginations to add their own creative visions.

Another dePaola-illustrated book that encourages imaginative thinking through its somewhat open-ended conclusion is *Nicholas Bentley Stoningpot III*, written by Ann McGovern.[8] A could-be counterpart to *Marianna May and Nursey*, this rich-boy tale, which features a highly individualized protagonist, could well have been penned by dePaola himself and surely makes him the right person to illustrate the offbeat adventure. DePaola's airy colors, friendly-looking animals, and amusing costumes project a lightheartedness that balances any concern that a boy-on-his-own story might give.

In true dePaola fashion, the illustrator sets the scene in the front matter, with Nicholas approaching a chauffeur-driven, 1920s vintage car piled high with luggage; boarding a sleek yacht; and putting out to sea. The text then takes up the story, telling how a "bored, bored, bored" Nicholas gets his wish for adventure when a violent storm strands him on a deserted island. In tandem with the narrative, the illustrator supplies a bright-colored parrot, two companionable goats, and a smiling monkey that accompany Nicky as he happily sets about building a hut, finding food, and gathering debris from drifting cargo. Totally entranced with his new life, Nicky dons a variety of disguises—which dePaola burlesques to the hilt—when rescue boats come near. One is that of a pirate, complete with mustache, earring, and sword. And while Nicky does build a raft— "one day he might want to leave Monkey Island and go back to the real world"—the book closes with the boy and his animal friends in silhouette,

cozily clustered under a palm-framed full moon. The text reads, "But not yet. Not for a long, long time."

Another dePaola collaborator is Nancy Willard; his illustrations for her quirky tale *The Mountains of Quilt* deserve close inspection as they come nearest to the colors and shapes found in much of his non-book art. While familiar elements are evident—floating stars, strong curved lines, pleasing shapes—the total look is different: DePaola employs the entire page, often encircling the text and placing small fanciful figures in soft colors against white space broken up with fluid sketchy lines. The result is whimsical and entirely in keeping with Willard's wry tale. The artist also has fun with the theme, designing quilts in a more chimerical way than used in *The Quilt Story* or *The Night Before Christmas*.

Quilts, pancakes, popcorn—what is important to dePaola often surfaces in his books, so to find quilts or food integrated into his art and stories is no surprise. Food is secondary, dePaola is quick to affirm; story comes first. And story continues to play an important role even in his nonfiction books.

The artist plays with space, form, color, and line, creating an apt backdrop for Willard's dreamlike story. *The Mountains of Quilt*

## "Tomie, Where Do You Get Your Ideas?"
### By Tomie dePaola

One of the first questions I get asked by children and grown-ups is, "Where do you get your ideas?" The answer I give is, "I don't really know. I guess they ultimately come from inside myself." All my characters seem to be parts of me, even Helga and Strega Nona. But what releases these ideas and characters is still a mystery to me. It can be one of those "lightbulb" situations like in the comic strips, or sometimes just plain tedious coaxing. Or sometimes it's a piece of music, a painting, an old photograph, or even a cup of coffee.

*Marianna May* came from looking at an old photograph of my mother all dressed up with a huge bow in her hair; *The Night of Las Posadas* from watching this beautiful Mexican tradition carried out when I visited New Mexico one Christmas; and *The Hunter and the Animals* from a day when I was home, leafing through Tamas Hofer's *Hungarian Folk Art.*[9]

I was simply struck by this reproduction of a Hungarian painted-wood panel—by its intricacy of pattern. It kept going through my mind, and eventually I used it as the basis for a wordless story about a lost hunter who is rescued by the forest animals and in thanksgiving breaks his gun in half. To the stylized patterns, I added my own measure of color and detail through the acorn-laden trees and the band of animals that peek through the foliage.

But whenever an idea or character is ready to jump out, I'd better be ready to grab it. Then it's just good, old-fashioned hard work to take the idea and make it work. No magic involved, just hard work, some luck, a good editor, and a lot of love on my part.

When I was in Italy for my first Bologna book fair, I met Leo Lionni, which was a genuine thrill. Over dinner one night, he lowered his voice and asked me, "Do you ever worry you don't have any more ideas?" It was wonderful to hear that fear, which many an author or artist has, expressed. "Of course I do," I told him. "But I have a trick. I always try to come up with a new project before I finish the one I'm working on. Sort of like sourdough bread—you take a little dough to start your new batch."

Then, too, I try to stay open to ideas. When children ask me, which they often do, where I get my ideas, I tell them from everywhere. It's a question of being open, receptive—like an empty cup. Of course, not every idea is a good one. The boring ones usually go quietly away, and it helps to have good editorial feedback.

*The Knight and the Dragon* actually came from a reading-promotion poster I had done for the American Library Association. It had hung on my studio wall for months when suddenly a kernel of an idea popped out, which eventually became the story and art you see today.

As for the Bill and Pete stories, their genesis is an article I read in *National Geographic* about the natural symbiotic relationship between the crocodile and the Egyptian plover. The whole idea amused me, and I began to create some stories about these two unlikely friends. Originally, there were three individual tales, but as my editor [Margaret Frith] and I worked through the idea, it seemed better to integrate them into one story. *Bill and Pete* was the result, and when it proved popular, I wrote two more.

"The world is full of sounds." *Sound*

# Informational Books

Most of dePaola's efforts from 1965 to 1973 were focused on illustrating other people's works—many of which were nonfiction. And at the time, dePaola maintains, that was enough. He was thrilled just to be involved in his life's dream—illustrating books for children. Even these early efforts display the beginnings of dePaola's now-matured and familiar style: a strong sense of design; integration of animals into the scenes; side touches of humor; cognizance of space; and decorative use of birds, stars, and suns.

While following a similar pattern, his work reflected his steady growth as an illustrator, with a gradual decline in cross-hatching, the emergence of a lighter and a more fluid line, and a general solidification of his own style. And the artwork he did for Peter Cohen's *Authorized Autumn Charts of the Upper Red Canoe River Country* depicts a keen awareness, for example, of the child reader. His early books also show diversity long before political correctness set in and a great sense of fun.

Threading comedy into informational books through text and pictures has been dePaola's highly welcomed contribution to the genre. In evaluating Lisa's Miller's *Sound,* James Eichner's *The Cabinet of the President of the United States,* Eleanor Boylan's *How to Be a Puppeteer,* and Beryl and Sam Epstein's *Who Needs Holes?* and *Pick It Up,* reviewers gave dePaola high marks for injecting humor into the books through his line

Sound waves move through different kinds of solids at different speeds. Sometimes, they have a hard time getting through at all.

Sound passes through air at a speed of about 1,130 feet every second. In water, it travels much faster; in solids, faster yet.

In *Sound*, dePaola's first book, a rabbit and a cat that conduct experiments, children at play, and a bird on the snowman's hat depict his early use of humor to convey information.

drawings, although one unknown critic found the art in *Sound,* dePaola well remembers, "far too imaginative for a science book."[1]

With *"Charlie Needs a Cloak,"* dePaola convincingly demonstrated his ability to provide straightforward information about an everyday subject (making a cloak) and to lift it above the ordinary through witty pencil drawings. By featuring one black-faced sheep, cantankerous but nevertheless enamored with Charlie, among a flock of passive white ones, dePaola creates a secondary character that works as a marvelous foil to Charlie's cloak-making efforts. The sheep's expressive face, capped with a beguiling set of frilly eyelashes, nudges the humor forward. The animal's elation in a bubble bath, embarrassment over a newly shorn body, determination to outpull Charlie in a tug-of-war over yarn, and numerous ploys to get the herder's attention resonate through the pictures; meanwhile, the text concerns itself strictly with Charlie's labors. A draft of this manuscript (then titled *Sebastian's Red Cloak*[2]), shows Charlie with a wife, but dePaola wisely decided that the story would be simpler—and stronger—if it revolved around just the shepherd and his sheep. It also gives Charlie more of an any-age persona. A rough sketch also includes an image depicting the sheep blissfully piling into bed with the shepherd—alongside which runs dePaola's pencil notes to himself, "cut bed, loom on left, Charlie facing gutter blissfully weaving, sheep 'weaving' woven fabric, modeling it."

DePaola employs three noteworthy techniques in this book, ones that he has used successfully in various titles since: the introduction of the plot in the front matter, the use of sequence illustration (which has roots in his love of film and comic books), and the inclusion of a visual extra.

Prior to the title page, villagers view a ragged-cloaked Charlie and one black-faced sheep standing on a hillside above the rest of the flock. The text reads, "Charlie was a shepherd. He had a cozy house, a big hat, a crook, and a flock of fat sheep. But everyone said . . ." On the next page, the words "Charlie needs a cloak" complete the sentence and, in a nifty sleight of hand, provide the title for the book.

While this design factor seems innocuous in comparison with the wackily designed publications of the 1990s, such as the Jon Scieszka-Lane Smith collaborations,[3] it was faulted by the judges in the 1975 Children's Book Showcase catalog.[4] "Elements felt to be less felicitous were: the drawing, which seemed to lack a certain finesse; the incorporation of the title page and copyright information within the body of the text." The book was, however, admired for "the variety and movement that carries the reader from interesting spread to spread throughout the book," as well as for its "well-placed type, for its controlled and judicious use of negative space, and for its humor."

The formal text, which begins "Poor Charlie! He really needed a new cloak," is accompanied by an image showing the reason for the shepherd's condition: a black-faced sheep contentedly chewing on Charlie's tattered garment. This scene also sets up the amusing ending: the sheep nibbling once more—this time on Charlie's brand new cloak! A circular story cleverly mapped out.

A fine example of a dePaola sequential action scene takes place during the shearing: On a double-page spread, the black-faced sheep apprehensively notes what is going on; races up a hill with Charlie in pursuit; grapples with the determined shepherd; is overpowered and sheared; and is last seen with only his head sticking out of the bushes in embarrassment. This treatment of events heightens the humor and capsulizes the action.

The visual extra that dePaola includes in *Charlie* quietly unfolds in the lower portions of the double-page spreads. Sharp-eyed viewers will spy a small gray mouse carrying away items often connected with Charlie's tasks (scissors during the sheep-shearing scene, red berries while Charlie dyes the wool, a ruler as Charlie measures the material). The

Staged throughout the story, these three vignettes amusingly portray Charlie's on-going plight with his sheep. *"Charlie Needs a Cloak"*

shepherd, however, is completely oblivious to the creature's activities. At the story's close, the mouse's maneuvers become clear—a small drawing of a cozy tentlike structure reveals its complete cache.

The success of *"Charlie Needs a Cloak"* encouraged dePaola to embark on other nonfictional titles, which followed a similar entertainment-with-information pattern. *The Cloud Book,* the first of a quintet for Holiday House,[5] sets the tone with a combination of fact (in the narrative) and humor (in the art), although the parts are not as well integrated as in the later titles. The pink-pajamaed, top-hatted youngster who introduces the subject of clouds on the cover and opening two pages suddenly disappears, with a resulting loss in continuity. Nevertheless, amusing images back dePaola's comparisons of clouds with mares' tails and cauliflowers, ultrabrief retellings of myths inspired by cloud shapes, and off-beat

interpretations of old weather sayings such as "He's in a fog" and "She has her head in the clouds."

*The Quicksand Book*, like *"Charlie Needs a Cloak,"* uses the front matter to lead into the story: From a ledge near her tree house, Jungle Girl merrily sails through the trees, only to have her vine break mid-leap, landing her in quicksand on the first page of the story. This device imaginatively opens the dialogue between Jungle Girl and Jungle Boy, who, in response to her call for help, blithely discusses the composition of quicksand and gives rescue procedures in the form of graphs and charts. Here too, the illustrations feature a visual extra: This time a monkey sets up a table for tea. While the mouse incident in *"Charlie Needs a Cloak"* played out separately, dePaola refines the extra escapade in *Quicksand.* He brings the monkey into the main story, which culminates

121

DO YOU KNOW WHERE QUICKSAND CAN BE FOUND? NO? WELL, I'LL TELL YOU. THE MOST COMMON FORM OF QUICKSAND IS FOUND ALONG THE SHORES AND IN THE BEDS OF SLOW RIVERS AND STREAMS THAT HAVE UNDERGROUND SPRINGS, JUST LIKE WHERE YOU ARE.

with Jungle Girl and the monkey enjoying tea and cakes, while Jungle Boy, now the one mired in the quicksand, shouts for assistance. The back of the dust jacket, however, ensures young readers that all is well—the three characters perch happily together on a rope swing.

While dePaola's theatrical tendencies emerge in many of his works, his use of jungle foliage as a proscenium arch and his positioning of the action from a single point of view make this title an early and excellent example of that influence. This technique also allows smooth juxtaposition of characters for their dialogue exchange, and the placement of Jungle Boy's charts at "stage right" is remindful of the signboards used

on the vaudeville stage. To avoid the stagnation that could result from the single viewpoint, the artist varies his scenes with the appearances of different animals (elephants, frogs, snakes, lions, turtles) and with the monkey's tea-making antics.

In answering the often-asked question "Why a book on quicksand?" dePaola replies, "Growing up, I was infatuated with Tarzan movies, and as a small child, I was warned to stay away from a nearby brook—supposedly there was quicksand." He then quickly gives credit to a librarian who sent him a letter from her Hawaiian grandson who asked for information about quicksand. Obviously a dePaola fan, the boy (who called himself Stevem [sic]) seemed to think that if his grandmother was a librarian then surely she knew the artist and suggested that she could have "Tomie dePaola write me one." DePaola quickly complied, and the book is dedicated to "Stevem and his grandmother." The research was difficult, dePaola says with a chuckle: "There is hardly anything available; I think I've written the definitive volume on the subject." When the book was published, Holiday House received a telegram saying, "Stevem is ecstatic and is whipping up a batch of quicksand and the dedication has me swinging from a cloud."[6]

DePaola includes directions for making quicksand. This kind of added touch is found also in the form of a simple story in *The Cloud Book*, two popcorn recipes in *The Popcorn Book*, a list of cat facts in *The Kids' Cat Book*, and directions for creating a tree ornament in *The Family Christmas Tree Book*. The idea for including these pieces derived, dePaola says, from his interest as a child in making things. Although such devices are now common, they were unusual at the time of *Quicksand's* publication.

In addition to the visual quips in *The Popcorn Book*, humor also is embedded in the dialogue as tousled-haired twins Tiny and Tony and their two identical cats sashay across the pages. While Tiny gives instructions

Dialogue balloons, containing both drawings and words, proves a satisfying and effective way to relay the art of corn popping to young readers. *The Popcorn Book*

for making popcorn, Tony supplies information about its history and relates anecdotes about its popularity—both of which are illustrated in balloons set off nicely from the ongoing story. When Tiny enthusiastically puts too many kernels in the pan, the twins experience an explosion of popcorn in the kitchen—but no matter, because, as they say, "The best thing about popcorn is eating it!" As the popcorn tumbles up, down, and everywhere, children quickly will see a connection to *Strega Nona*.

Harmony between picture and text is clearly in evidence in *Popcorn*, but once again it's the story element that makes these informational titles appealing to children and critically satisfying to adults. DePaola's concern for story, about reaching down into his four-year-old child self, carries over into the creation of his collections, where traces of story often can be found in the illustrations, tying the book neatly together.

"Old Mother Goose / When she wanted to wander /
Would ride through the air / On a very fine gander."
*Tomie dePaola's Mother Goose*

# Mother Goose and Other Collections

Story is evident in *Tomie dePaola's Mother Goose* from the very beginning. In the front matter, several images feature a young boy and girl reading on a pillowed bench. In the first one, the duo appear as bookends; above is a picture of a goose. The half-title page rearranges these images: The girl is now reading aloud to the boy, who is holding a stuffed white goose in his hands; the goose picture has been replaced by a window looking out to billowing clouds. To complete the connection, the final illustration shows the two children fast asleep, the book spread open on the girl's lap. In the sky above, Mother Goose, in silhouette, sails off across a full moon.

One-time bookstore owner and advocate of children's literature Robert Hale discussed this prevalent dePaola technique in *The Horn Book Magazine.*[1] Hale pointed out the straw-hatted, blue-jacketed boy who keeps turning up—either having many of the adventures described in the rhymes or observing them with deep interest—as a fellow journeyer sharing the fun, and he mentions a perky-eared Airedale and a number of different cats doing the same. In *Tomie dePaola's Book of Poems,* a sailboat provides the stimulus, smoothly leading into the opening poem—Emily Dickinson's "There Is No Frigate Like a Book."[2] This kind of visual interplay is typical dePaola: a concern for aesthetic unity that is completely within a child's reach.

This connection between child appeal and artistry continues on the title page in Mother Goose, where a smiling, bonneted woman is seen beckoning to a large white bird. Juxtaposed with the first page of text is Mother Goose in flight on the goose's back, hand waving. Come along, she seems to say, this reading adventure is about to begin.

The creation of this 128-page collection happened in a roundabout way. Editor Margaret Frith arrived in New Hampshire for a work session one spring in the early 1980s. She walked into dePaola's studio and saw five Mother Goose paintings pinned to the wall, which the artist had just completed for the upcoming Illustrators' Exhibition at the Children's Book Fair in Bologna, Italy.[3] Struck with the imaginative spirit of the renderings, Frith immediately suggested that dePaola think about creating a Mother Goose book, to which dePaola replied, "Oh, sure, Margaret, the world really needs another Mother Goose." Frith's answer was "But, Tomie, there is no Tomie Mother Goose." Several weeks later, the idea was revitalized when dePaola's London editor Joy Backhouse[4] saw the five illustrations in Bologna and suggested turning the artwork into accordion-folded story streamers depicting four Mother Goose verses, and publishing them as a joint venture between Methuen (her company) and Putnam. In 1984 *Tomie dePaola's Mother Goose Story Streamers* was released on both sides of the Atlantic with *Tomie dePaola's Mother Goose* making its appearance the following year. Coincidentally, it launched dePaola's celebration of his twentieth year in publishing.

However, with hundreds of Mother Goose books available in libraries, new ones coming daily onto the market, and still others that remain fresh in people's memories—how does one go about making a new rendition unique? "The design factor" is how dePaola characterized it when explaining the process that he, Frith, and then Putnam art director Nanette Stevenson[5] worked through to bring to completion the large-format, full-color edition that became *Tomie dePaola's Mother Goose*.

In doing the research, dePaola read every edition of every verse he could find. But when making his selections, he used, wherever possible, the classic verses collected by English folklorists Peter and Iona Opie. He also took to heart their advice in *The Oxford Nursery Rhyme Book*,[6] which suggests that any Mother Goose for young children needed to have not only each rhyme illustrated but every stanza of the longer rhymes as well. With this in mind, dePaola and Frith worked closely together, winnowing the choices carefully to allow for the "open and light" format that dePaola wanted. Their goal was to include a mix of well-known verses as well as less-familiar fare. To give variety on another level, they categorized their selections into kinds of verse: four-line,

long, narrative, nonsense rhymes, and so forth. For the illustrations, dePaola "used a dark brown line to delineate the stylized figures and settings, concentrating on simple shapes and clarity of composition."[7]

In the meantime, Stevenson constructed a grid, mapping out the book page by page, to ensure a natural flow and harmony. As a result, images appear in double-page, single-page, or half-page spreads; as vertical borders; or as individual spots that sometimes surround, sometimes adjoin, but always give both variety and unity to the book.

Peopled with the young, the elderly, and the in between from a variety of cultures, dePaola's Mother Goose characters of old reflect the diversity of today's world.

Once the grid was established and the selections were firm, an in-house designer joined the team. At this point, decisions were made as to size and kind of type, placement of text, and width of margins, and thought was given to special design situations. After the rhymes were typeset and sent to dePaola, he began the artwork. Pencil sketches were completed, fit into the designated art areas, and checked for size and balance. Finally, the painting of the more than three hundred full-color illustrations could begin. Which image did he start with? "I wanted," dePaola explained, "to establish the image of Mother Goose on the dust jacket, which the marketing department needed for catalog copy and to start work on the publicity. It was important to me that even though you don't see Mama Goose (my nickname for the spry lady) throughout the book, her presence be identified. We (Margaret and I) discussed at length whether she should be seen in profile (my preference) or in full face (Margaret's choice); you can see who won! I did get my way on the title page, where you see Mother Goose complete with finger pointing outward, an image I remembered from an early version in my childhood."[8]

The *Mother Goose* team's time and efforts were rewarded: With more than 300,000 hardback copies in print (as of this writing) and still selling, the book is now considered a classic in the Mother Goose genre.[9] Mother Goose herself is a winner. She has enough homespun attributes (glasses, gray hair, apron, and buckled shoes) to play the part, while her dapper attire (driving gloves, a debonair hat trimmed with a long, curling feather, and bright red stockings) gives her class.

DePaola's color choices—clear pinks, violets, blues, goldenrods, and teal greens—glow against pure white space, allowing the comic undertones room to flourish. Diversity of character is evident: Faces with almond eyes, mocha complexions, and tightly curled black hair shine from the pages along with pink cheeks and blond braids. And there is

Hot cross buns, hot cross buns;
One a penny poker,
Two a penny tongs,
Three a penny fire shovel,
Hot cross buns.

Baa, baa, black sheep,
    Have you any wool?
Yes, sir, yes, sir,
    Three bags full;
One for the master,
    And one for the dame,
And one for the little boy
    Who lives down the lane.

The cock's on the roof top
    Blowing his horn,
The bull's in the barn
    A-threshing the corn,
The maids in the meadow
    Are making the hay,
The ducks in the river
    Are swimming away.

diversity in the presentation as well. Some of the rhymes are depicted in a straightforward manner ("Rub-a-dub-dub" shows three men in a tub), while others exhibit an inventive dimension ("The cat goes fiddle-i-fee" has each visual vignette growing larger as the cumulative verse grows longer, and a white-sided barn serves as setting for both "Baa, baa, black sheep" and "The cock's on the rooftop").

In his discussion of *Tomie dePaola's Mother Goose,* Hale went on to say, "In the theater, the trick is to make the words appear as if that is the first time they were ever spoken. In this book because of dePaola's approach, there is that feeling of first time. How nice to have the feeling of first time commingled with one's own memories of rhymes and rhythms, to have surprise as well as recognition—and to have it all in rich colors that are closer than ever before to the artist's originals."[10]

The upswing of popularity for board books in 1997 motivated Putnam to choose thirty-two verses from the collection and issue them in a compact five-by-seven-inch, thick-paged format. Renamed *Tomie's Little Mother Goose,* it introduced this ageless woman—and dePaola—to a new audience of even younger readers.[11]

Two separate verses are cleverly linked through one black-roofed barn.

131

Then she said, "Who will help me eat the bread?"
"Oh! I will," said the duck.
"Oh! I will," said the cat.
"Oh, I will," said the dog.
"Oh, no, you won't!" said the Little Red Hen. "I and my chicks will." And she called her chicks and shared the bread with them.

In 1986, dePaola reprised his success with *Mother Goose* with another collection—*Tomie dePaola's Favorite Nursery Tales*. A wraparound dust jacket features a boy reading aloud to two other children amid an assortment of teddy bears and dolls, and the artist references his earlier book with a hanging picture of Mother Goose on the back of the jacket. The toys share spot images throughout the book, along with the Airedale, whose ears, Hale once claimed, "are more expressive than most people's faces."[12]

For this book, dePaola relied on selections his mother shared with him as a child. The dedication, in fact, reads, "To my mother, Flossie Downey dePaola, whose lap I sat on a long time ago, and listened to her tell me many of these stories." The choices from mostly familiar sources—Joseph Jacobs, Aesop, the Brothers Grimm, Hans Christian Andersen, and P. C. Asbjörnsen—are told with wit and warmth and presented with panache. The pointy-eared, redheaded, mischievous-looking elves ("The Elves and the Shoemaker"), the haughtily clothed—and unclothed—emperor ("The Emperor's New Clothes"), the long-nosed, ogle-eyed green troll ("The Three Billy-Goats Gruff"), and Little Red Hen's disdainful silly friends ("The Little Red Hen") have a spirit all their own.

DePaola's next ventures as anthologist came in quick succession over a five-year period: *Tomie dePaola's Book of Christmas Carols, Tomie dePaola's Book of Poems,* and *Tomie dePaola's Book of Bible Stories* (the Old Testament section of which was reissued in 1995 by popular demand as *Tomie dePaola's Book of the Old Testament*). Each of these collections required extensive collaboration between dePaola, Frith, and Stevenson, and often involved others such as designer Patrick Collins and editors Arthur Levine and Nora Cohen.[13]

The five anthologies required the choosing or retelling of hundreds of selections, the creation of nearly a thousand full-color pieces of art, the preparation of grids for and design of more than six hundred pages of text, the planning of front and back matter (endpapers, title pages, dust jackets, book casings, and indexes), and the coordination of all these aspects through the production process. All of these anthologies contain distinctive dePaola trademarks: luminescent use of color; strong sense of balance between text, image, and white space; recurring folk motifs and attention to the constrictions of bookmaking. These patterns and techniques, which surface throughout dePaola's work, have been the subject of criticism. Yet for those who take the time to explore carefully, the visual themes and motifs he employs not only add dimension but by their very presence give special identity to his illustrations.

In "Pharaoh's Daughter Finds Moses," dePaola's vibrant teal blues frame the focal image of baby Moses in the floating basket. *Tomie dePaola's Book of Bible Stories*

"The people said good-bye to Francis, their brother, their saint,
the poor man of Assisi." *Francis, the Poor Man of Assisi*

# Patterns, Visual Themes, and Motifs

A close reading and studying of dePaola's books illuminates the visual themes, patterns, and motifs he incorporates into his work. While many of these elements have been pointed out earlier, their meanings, relationships to his life, and impacts on his work become clearer when addressed as a whole. Partially because of these symbols, dePaola is recognized far beyond the children's book world by book collectors, seekers of religious titles, devotees of folkloric objets d'art, and appreciators of whimsy. While these aficionados find their own connections to the white birds, hearts, stars, moons, Welsh terriers, Airedales, rabbits, and cats that grace dePaola's pages—sometimes as decorations, sometimes as integral aspects of illustrations—dePaola says that for him these symbols have both an artistic and a personal significance.

So closely is dePaola associated with these symbols that when he doesn't include them, reviewers are likely to note their absence. Yet inclusion has also brought reproof that his illustrations "all look alike." That criticism may come, in part, because of the wrongful notion that these figures appear in all of the artist's books. They aren't found in his autobiographical tales at all, and, in fact, are never used indiscriminately. "I include them when the story calls for a highly stylized technique, such as in *Francis, the Poor Man of Assisi*; when there is enough latitude for a visual joke, such as in *Marianna May and Nursey*; or when there is

room for graphic elaboration, such as in *The Story of the Three Wise Kings.* There I deliberately painted the Mother and Child, for example, in a traditional Romanesque-style pose referred to as 'Seat of Wisdom, Throne of Justice.'"

His personal menagerie of animals has changed over the years, and so have the animals appearing in his books. In his early career, dePaola had a Schnauzer, seen romping about the background of *Finders Keepers, Losers Weepers*; later he owned cats—Satie among them—that have enjoyed starring roles in *The Kids' Cat Book, Songs of the Fog Maiden,* and *Bonjour, Mr. Satie* and have made other cameo appearances; Airedales are spotlighted in *Tomie dePaola's Mother Goose* and Jill Bennett's *Teeny Tiny*; and his Welsh terriers clamor for places in books such as Arnold Shapiro's *Mice Squeak, We Speak.* And the rabbits? "Well," dePaola remarks with a grin, "they just show up."

White birds have, undoubtedly, become the motif most associated with dePaola, and he uses them liberally. Although the white bird didn't appear in its current form until the 1970s, birds as decorative objects—along with suns and stars—can be found in books as far back as *Sound.* Their shapes and colorings have been refined, of course, and now readers, especially children, often seek them out as assurance that a title is indeed a dePaola book. And Whitebird has become, as mentioned earlier, the name of dePaola's business enterprise.

A multicultural cast of child angels includes one holding her own winged kitten; stylized elements decorate and embellish but never intrude on the scene.
*Country Angel Christmas*

136

The stars, suns, and moons, particularly those in his Christmas stories, have a religious connotation, as dePaola pointed out in an interview in the *Concord Monitor*.[1] "The six-pointed stars, for example, in *The Legend of Old Befana* and in *The Story of the Three Wise Kings,* symbolize the star of creation; the five-pointed stars the Incarnation; the panther seen with the three kings in *The Story of the Three Wise Kings* symbolizes the way true believers are drawn to Christ; and the oak tree is an image of strength."

"Hearts," according to dePaola, "crept into my art years ago and have stayed there out of habit." During the flower-child era of the 1960s, his apprenticeship with liturgical artist Corita Kent[2] often was marked with heart decorations. It seemed natural, dePaola says, to incorporate the heart shape into many of his pictures and into his signature. Beginning with his 1982 books, a small heart almost always appears on his cover art. Then, in the midst of a three-hour autographing session at the Tattered Cover bookstore in Denver, he stopped signing his last name; some time later, at an American Library Association conference, in what dePaola describes as a pivotal moment in his career, he decided to appropriate the combined heart-Tomie pen stroke as his "official" signature.

Tradition is important to dePaola, so it is no surprise to find images of his familiar characters woven into his books. Charlie, from *"Charlie Needs a Cloak,"* like Strega Nona, has become somewhat of a dePaola icon. The stalwart shepherd can be found tucked into a variety of the artist's books: a lamb's doll in *Haircuts for the Woolseys,* a traveler in *The Cloud Book,* a dream image in *Songs of the Fog Maiden.* His likeness

A midnight-blue sky nicely offsets the glow surrounding the Holy Family, bringing a quiet dignity to this image for "Once in Royal David's City." *Tomie dePaola's Book of Christmas Carols*

*Days of the Blackbird*, TOP; *Mice Squeak, We Speak*, CENTER; and *Tony's Bread*, BOTTOM, are but three examples of how placement of hands can supply expression.

appears as the main character in dePaola's retelling of the Aesop fable *The Wind and the Sun*; the 1995 rerelease featured a much more prominent Charlie on the cover—a sure sign of the shepherd's lasting popularity.

Neither is Strega Nona shy about demanding her share of recognition: One can find her in a picture on the wall in *The Wuggie Norple Story* and in *I Love You, Mouse*; as a memento of the grown-up Tommy's work in *The Art Lesson*; and as a figure in *Tomie dePaola's Mother Goose*. In another example, an Italian-style Pierrot turns up in *The Clown of God*. But more interesting are the precursors that have materialized. *The Tiger and the Rabbit,* the second book he illustrated, written by Pura Belpré, includes Strega Nona and Manuela (from *Alice Nizzy Nazzy*) look-alikes; and, long before the character Tommy made his first auto-biographical appearance, "self portraits" began showing up in *Odd Jobs and Friends, Joe and the Snow,* and other stories.

Another recurring device is dePaola's positioning of the human hand. This pattern sometimes can be attributed to the influence of pre-Renaissance art, where the hand often is given visual prominence; at other times dePaola uses the technique to portray character (Big Anthony), provide expression (*Days of the Blackbird*), energize the action (*Sing, Pierrot, Sing*), direct the eye (*The Quilt Story*), complete a composition (*Tony's Bread*), or balance an image (*The Friendly Beasts*). Especially striking examples can be noted on the cover of *Francis, the Poor Man of Assisi,* in a spread from *An Early American Christmas,* and on the title page of Shapiro's *Mice Squeak, We Speak,* which depicts six upheld hands, each holding a tiny mouse.

DePaola also enjoys including visual jokes in his work. Examples range from a boy reading a magic book upside down in Patricia MacLachlan's *Moon, Stars, Frogs, and Friends*; to the appearance of a medieval bookmobile in *The Knight and the Dragon*; to drawings of Puss in Boots, The Owl and the Pussycat, and other literary cats in *The Kids' Cat Book*; to a picture of a suitcase labeled "Dad" in *Bill and Pete*. In *Helga's Dowry,* a cloud sporting one eye, à la the god Odin, and three billy-goats gruff look-alikes peering over a bridge display dePaola's mischievous joy in graphic jokes. Further evidence can be found in an accompanying note on a Kerlan-held early sketch for *Big Anthony and the Magic Ring*[3] that says "Big Anthony—leaning like man in Millet's *The Angelus.*"[4] DePaola says, "If readers see them, that's great—and many kids relish finding them. If not, that is okay too; I know they are there."

The artist's thespian predilections, carried through from childhood and extended by his teaching and work both onstage and behind the curtain, carry heavy influence. He, in fact, recommends that anyone interested in illustrating children's books have an "avid love of theater." As he points out: "An illustrator must cast the play, costume the characters, plan their entrances and exits, design the setting, and move the main action forward—all while not losing sight of the overall plot." A proscenium arch often frames dePaola's images, a highly noticeable effect in *The Quicksand Book.* And one can almost imagine sitting in an audience and watching the scenes in *The Triumphs of Fuzzy Fogtop* or *Watch Out for the Chicken Feet in Your Soup* play out on dePaola's "stage," where backgrounds have the feel of a set, the dialogue happens center stage, and the viewpoint is from a single perspective.

Overhanging leaves form a proscenium arch, framing the droll theatrics of this muddling twosome. *The Triumphs of Fuzzy Fogtop*

The man folded his newspaper.
"Oh, you've changed, Harry. You have, no use denying it. That full head of hair, where has it gone? You're bald as an egg now, Harry."

This theatrical influence can be seen in other books as well: A group of children put on a Nativity play in *The Christmas Pageant,* Old Mother Hubbard's story is presented as a theatrical production in *The Comic Adventures of Old Mother Hubbard and Her Dog,* and Jack and Jill appear as marionette figures in *Tomie dePaola's Mother Goose.*

On the first page of *The Knight and the Dragon,* the knight appears in the window of a medieval tower, while the dragon peers from the rounded opening of his cave; Mary is first glimpsed through an open barn door in *Mary Had a Little Lamb;* Strega Nona often oversees the goings-on of Calabria from the window of her small house; in *The Legend of Old Befana,* Befana's first appearance is in an arched doorway; in *Pages of Music,* a villager watches from a window as the protagonist and his mother arrive on the isle of Sardinia; and on the cover of *What the Mailman Brought,* William looks out through his sickroom window. Not only does this device bring attention to the character and ready the child for the tale within, but it also emphasizes dePaola's cognizance of story and the need to draw young readers into the action through character.

Immediate identification of character with setting results when dePaola frames a knight in his tower, a dragon in its cave, and Mary in an old New England-style barn. *The Knight and the Dragon* and *Mary Had a Little Lamb*

This importance of narrative also surfaces in the artist's inclusion of the visual extras that unfold in his artwork. Three well-known examples are the mouse story from *"Charlie Needs a Cloak,"* the tea-setting scene in *The Quicksand Book,* and, in *Helga's Dowry,* the Troll King's lurking around the sides of the action long before he makes an appearance near the story's end. In an early book, Mary Calhoun's *Old Man Whickutt's Donkey,* dePaola used the mechanism well, injecting an amusing graphic sideshow involving a crow that busily eats the corn

DePaola delights in visual secrets; here, the artist "hides" the Troll King away from Helga's eyes but puts her upfront in the picture for young readers to see. *Helga's Dowry*

that a miller is taking to the mill. "Sometimes," dePaola comments, "children see these asides before adults do. I recall a friend telling me about showing *Helga's Dowry* to three children who had spotted the Troll King hiding throughout the pictures; she, however, thought he had just appeared suddenly at the very end of the story. The reason children see these details is that they are often more visually perceptive—a situation that needs to be encouraged before they grow older and, sadly, lose that ability."[5]

DePaola may not have been the first to weave a "secret" story into his pictures, but he was surely one of the earlier illustrators to do so. He was also one of the first to use the front matter to tantalize his readers. Prime examples are *Watch Out for the Chicken Feet in Your Soup*, in which Joey warns his friend Eugene about his eccentric grandmother; and Elizabeth Winthrop's *Maggie and the Monster*, in which, on the

The vertical trim size of *Days of the Blackbird* fits the upward sweep of the mountains, while the three-part journey by ship, train, and car in *Bonjour, Mr. Satie* is best accommodated in a horizontal format.

half-title page, a figure stealthily enters an open door, followed on the title page by a huge shadow skulking behind the big-eared, plaid-dressed green monster. Sometimes, as in *Days of the Blackbird,* dePaola uses the title page to place the story geographically, while in *Bonjour, Mr. Satie,* a journey (from Europe to Rosalie and Conrad's home) skillfully unfolds on the title-page spread. On the title page of *Tom,* dePaola introduces his characters through photographlike images, bringing about a nostalgic look.

Innovation has been a hallmark of dePaola's work in a number of areas. The inclusion of sources, a note on the evolution of a tale, or information on how he became aware of a story is found in many of dePaola's books. Although today it is a common practice, it was not when he provided source material for *The Lady of Guadalupe* and *The Legend of the Indian Paintbrush*, published in the 1980s. And, certainly unique at the time of publication, dialogue makes up the complete narrative in *Watch Out for the Chicken Feet in Your Soup* (1974).

His use of sequence illustration is also enterprising. In *Mary Had a Little Lamb*, for example, the lamb listens to Mary read in the attic, keeps her company while she works in the kitchen, and sleeps at the foot of her bed. The artist, however, is quick to assert that he did not "invent" the device; its use, he says, can be traced to medieval painters as well as to the work of Brueghel the Elder, and is found in the Bayeux Tapestry.[6]

The meaning of the familiar lines "And everywhere that Mary went, the lamb was sure to go" is intensified by a scene that shows the duo together at work, at play, and asleep. *Mary Had a Little Lamb*

Where does all this creativity come from? "When you've been in publishing as long as I have," dePaola remarks, "you try to vary your work to keep it fresh, while still keeping within your own style." With the year 2000 marking the thirty-fifth year of his publishing career, dePaola has indeed been in the profession a long time. "I've seen a lot of changes," he says. "What I don't see in new people coming up is a sense of their own vision. In some ways, there has been a loss of story—too many picture books today are merely portfolios of paintings. On the other hand, there is much for teachers and parents to choose from. Those looking to share books with children have a nearly endless variety of art styles, techniques, mediums, and palettes available—a great difference from what I had as a child."

"One summer day, Princess Dulcia was gathering seashells on the beach when she came upon a remarkable beast, the likes of which had never been seen before in Timlin." *The Wonderful Dragon of Timlin*

# Publishing History

When Florence Alexander came into dePaola's life, his career as a children's book illustrator took a decided turn in the direction he had long wanted to go. As often happens, this bit of fate came about through an odd chain of events. DePaola came to know Blanche Gregory,[1] a literary agent who handled adult authors, through a mutual friend. Gregory had decided to expand her business and rep a few illustrators, and at a cocktail party, she suggested that dePaola get a portfolio ready for review. Shortly after that, Gregory was elected president of the Agents' Guild,[2] a time-heavy commitment that precluded taking on any new clients. DePaola received the bad news when he went to Gregory's Manhattan office to show his portfolio; however, in a burst of kindness, Gregory called Alexander, who was an artists' agent, asking if she might be interested in this young talent. "Sure," dePaola remembers Alexander telling Gregory, "if he can get down to my office by noon." To echo Strega Nona—the rest is history.

His teaching load at Newton College in the Boston area at that time allowed him the flexibility to live in Manhattan, where he was close to publishers. Teaching gave him a small income as well as classroom experience, which proved to be especially important: "My efforts to verbalize my thoughts to students made me internalize my own work and philosophy about art to myself."

As his reputation grew, so did his work product. And in the mid-1960s, his own writing took seed. Bernice Kohn (later Hunt[3]), according to dePaola, was an early mentor. Not only was her own book *Sound* his first illustrating assignment, but also she was helpful when he wrote his own first story—the somewhat slight but nevertheless sweet *The Wonderful Dragon of Timlin.* This book has an interesting family connection: The title comes partially from the names of two of sister Maureen's children—Timolyne and Timothy, as the dedication, set in a heart, attests.

With his work becoming known and his connection with a supportive agent, dePaola felt free to head for California in the late 1960s. He spent more than four years in the City by the Bay. They were busy years, as he recalls, and the record proves it: He produced nearly thirty books. Although most were written by other people, he authored six books himself. He worked with editor Jeanne Vestal (Lippincott) on *Finders Keepers, Losers Weepers,* with Mary Russell (Bobbs-Merrill) on *The Wonderful Dragon of Timlin,* and with Eunice Holsaert (Hawthorn) on *Joe and the Snow.* "They were each extremely helpful and willing to give time and attention to a young writer and illustrator," dePaola recalls.

Prentice-Hall editor Ellen Roberts, who shepherded *Strega Nona* from that doodle on the drawing pad to Caldecott Honor Book, and Holsaert, who had moved to Holiday House, proved to be especially strong guiding forces. When dePaola moved back to the East Coast in 1971, Holsaert encouraged him to use the memories of his childhood to write his own stories. In an ironic turn of events, after helping him in the early stages of writing *Nana Upstairs & Nana Downstairs,* Holsaert declined the manuscript when it was finished. DePaola then submitted it to Barbara Lucas at Putnam, where the book was completed, garnered great reviews, and became an immediate success with children and critics alike.

His first book with Putnam, which had brought him into contact with Lucas, was *Rutherford T Finds 21B,* and when Lucas moved on to Harcourt, dePaola continued to work with her, publishing such books as *The Clown of God* and *Helga's Dowry.* Margaret Frith, who had been the in-house associate editor on the physical science series at Coward-McCann, then moved into Lucas's spot at Putnam, where she has been ever since, and she and dePaola began what has become a successful twenty-some year association. *Bill and Pete,* published in 1978, was their first collaboration as editor and artist-author.

When Lucas left Harcourt, dePaola worked with editor Maria Modugno, and after Holsaert left Holiday House, he developed a close working connection with John and Kate Briggs and editor Margery Cuyler. "With *Quicksand,*" dePaola remembers, "Margery encouraged me to be as humorous as possible—to just take it and run. We also shared a strong interest in religious themes. Holiday House allowed me to do *Francis, the Poor Man of Assisi* and *The Lady of Guadalupe* the way I wanted to do them, without forcing them into a commercial mode." It was under the Holiday House imprint that dePaola published many of his Christmas and religious titles as well as popular books such as *Mary Had a Little Lamb* and *The Hunter and the Animals.*[4] The latter, a wordless book with a distinct anti-hunting message, brought a bit of controversy from gun owners.

Brushes with censorship, however, have been few, and likewise, dePaola has come through another publishing hazard—the reviewing

To capture the quality of Hungarian folk art, which inspired *The Hunter and the Animals,* dePaola made important use of negative space. He drew images in thick brown-black line and used transparent colored inks to cover the page, emphasizing the many connecting shapes that determined the negative space of the background. Then, as a last step, he dry-brushed opaque tempera paint around the images, onto the background letting little pieces of color underneath show through.

process—more or less unscathed. That is not to say that he hasn't suffered a few slings and arrows. In reviewing *Francis, the Poor Man of Assisi* for *The New York Times Book Review*, adult author Mary Gordon[5] said she longed for a portrayal of Francis that was "a bit more ragged, a bit wilder, that the wolf looked a little less tame, the stigmata a bit more bloody." In reviewing *Quicksand*,[6] a critic suggested that Jungle Girl (rather than Jungle Boy) should have been the rescuer, and in *The New York Times Book Review*, David Macaulay,[7] a lone negative voice, called *The Art Lesson* "mediocre and self-indulgent." More often than not, however, the reviews have been in dePaola's favor, and he has racked up more stars, pointers, best books, children's choices, notables, and generally outstanding reviews than most of his contemporaries. His work also has generated numerous articles, interviews, and profiles, and he has gained more kudos, awards, recognitions, and honors than is feasible to list.

When technological advances in the printing industry allowed publishers to drop the preseparated art process[8] and reproduce illustrations directly from the original artwork, dePaola's work, along with other artists', could be better appreciated. It also allowed him to use the palette's full range and to experiment with color, shape, and texture. He could choose a style—from painterly to comic book to folk art—that fit the text rather than be bound by the restrictions of reproduction.

DePaola's publishing relationship with Holiday House ended only when he signed an exclusive global agreement with Putnam to be his one and only publisher. There have been exceptions. According to dePaola,

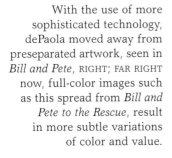

With the use of more sophisticated technology, dePaola moved away from preseparated artwork, seen in *Bill and Pete*, RIGHT; FAR RIGHT now, full-color images such as this spread from *Bill and Pete to the Rescue*, result in more subtle variations of color and value.

Frith and Putnam have been very understanding about allowing him some freedom with the contract. Nevertheless, the global agreement, the first in the industry for a children's book illustrator, is one he is proud of because, he feels, "it brought recognition and importance to all the children's book field." Peter Israel,[9] then CEO of Putnam, came to him with this global-agreement, exclusive-publisher idea at the time when *Tomie dePaola's Mother Goose* was about to be published. "It was," dePaola says with a chuckle, "a contract too good to refuse!" In another nod to his success, dePaola was the only children's book author mentioned in MCA's Circle of Assets in a *Newsweek*[10] article about Michael Ovitz and MCA, who at the time owned Putnam/Berkley.

In 1997, Putnam became part of Penguin Putnam, but the financial dealings at the top have not affected the long affiliation between dePaola and Frith. While they differ at times about details, they communicate almost daily by phone or fax, talking in shorthand and working closely together to bring about the best book possible. In speaking with each of them individually, it quickly becomes clear that they are, in fact, a mutual-admiration society.

The two have a schedule of books far into the twenty-first century and another list of "want-to" publishing ideas that will undoubtedly keep dePaola's many fans happy. Both are excited about new Strega Nona stories, more Irish and Italian folktales, picture books about Tommy, and especially more titles in the series 26 Fairmount Avenue—the place that harbors so many memories for dePaola of times long ago.

# Whitebird Books

In 1989, as part of dePaola's and Putnam's global agreement, Putnam launched a new imprint—Whitebird Books[11]—with dePaola as creative director. "Tomie wanted a new challenge," his editor Margaret Frith says, "and as a publisher of fine picture books, we at Putnam thought this would be a great extension of our publishing program. Through the years, Tomie has sent artists to us, has always generously advised new talent, has taught art, and his gravitation to the folktale genre made this a natural."

"The idea was," dePaola says, "to feature less-familiar folktales from around the world for children ages four to eight or nine." Little-known authors or illustrators were sometimes paired with established artists or authors, with dePaola doing some of the retellings or artwork himself. In an interesting turnaround, his retelling of *The Legend of the Persian Carpet* was accompanied with art by then-beginning illustrator Claire Ewart. Others to get their starts with Whitebird Books were Valerie Scho Carey (*Quail Song*), Warren Ludwig (*Good Morning, Granny Rose*), and Tony Griego (*The Green Gourd*). Some titles in the line carried familiar names such as Tony Johnston, who wrote *The Badger and the Magic Fan*, with dePaola's artwork, and others, such as *Tony's Bread*, dePaola wrote and illustrated himself. As creative director, dePaola also provided an individualized note about the tale at the beginning of each book.

In creating the line, dePaola says, "I didn't want to use my own name, so we decided on Whitebird, my personal symbol." DePaola's role was that of an acquisition editor. Manuscripts were sent to him for screening and selection, and sometimes he suggested promising work he found in the course of his speaking engagements and autographing tours around the country. Final manuscript and art decisions, however, were made when dePaola, Frith, and art director Nanette Stevenson sat down together.

"I was not involved in the line-by-line editing or in the production process," dePaola says, "I was more interested in the stories. I like folktales. And in the ones I like to tell, anyway, there's always some interesting message that a child can take away with him. My story *Jamie O'Rourke and the Big Potato* is a good example. The whole notion, which I just love, that a lazy man can end up on top, is wonderful. That would never happen in a fairy tale, which tends to rely on magic and the distinct forces of good and evil. In folktales, you can have the antihero getting all the goods."

Why did it fold? According to Frith, "The original idea behind the series was not only to publish folktales by Tomie but to introduce new authors and artists that he discovered. However, as we entered the 1990s, the picture book genre exploded and multicultural titles—especially folktales—began flooding the market; Whitebird Books was no longer unique. Except for Tomie's own books, it became more and more difficult to launch Whitebird titles and to build a backlist—and without a backlist the series lost its impetus. It was simply a sign of the times."

DePaola still maintains that "Whitebird Books was a great idea; over a five-year period we published ten titles featuring tales from Italy, Russia, Mexico, Peru, Switzerland, Korea, and the United States. The collection was in full color, was well designed, had a nice trim size—all in all it was very attractive."[12]

"Off he went, down the road, pleased that he had fixed the tower."
*Big Anthony, His Story*

# Creating the Book

DePaola's remark that Strega Nona went from doodle pad to book might give the impression that the illustrative process happens overnight. Nothing could be further from the truth. "Even before the writing begins," dePaola maintains, "a picture book sits in my head for long periods of time. Then, depending on its complexity and what else is happening in my life, it might take months to write. I usually work on several books at once—while I'm checking galleys for a spring book, for instance, I will be working on the art for a book to be published in the fall and sketching out ideas for a future title.

"My first impulse is to begin with the pictures, but I restrain myself, as I thoroughly believe that story must come first." And what makes a good story for children? DePaola answers quickly: "The same things that make a good story for adults: complexity, plot, character development, suspense, drama, humor, sadness. The only difference is that in a children's book, you have fewer words and more pictures."

Furthermore, he explains, the text space is very limited: A paragraph often has to be compressed into a single sentence. He has to be conscious of the way the words sound, because the book is likely to be read aloud to a child. After finishing the text, dePaola then prepares sketches, which often look like doodles, because, he says, "if my drawings are too complete, the final artwork dies." The actual drawings for a thirty-two-page picture book could take from six weeks up to three months to

DePaola's "Whitebird" takes over for the stork on the dedication page.

complete, while an extended book, such as Mother Goose, can take several years from creative seed to finished product.

As for his preferred art approach, dePaola says in *Children's Books and Their Creators*[1] that he uses one of several techniques. One is to build up "skins" of color, as in *The Art Lesson*; another is more painterly, such as he used in *Bonjour, Mr. Satie* and *Days of the Blackbird*; and a third is a combination of the two, for example, in *Hark! A Christmas Sampler* by Jane Yolen. What is important, he feels, is to choose a medium and technique appropriate to the story he is working on.

Following are the stages that dePaola, Frith, art director Cecilia Yung, designer Donna Mark,[2] and others went through to bring *Big Anthony, His Story*[3] to fruition. DePaola's willingness to allow sketches, changes,

P. 5    These things begin very early. In fact, when they passed little Anthony around the festive tables, so everyone could get a good look at the newest member of the family, little Anthony fell fast asleep.

"See," said grandma, "He doesn't pay attention. I don't know — little Anthony may be a bit of TROUBLE."

And was grandma right!

P. 6    Little Anthony began to grow.

"He's going to be a big boy," said Grampa.

"He takes after my side of the family" (all looking at grandpa who is very short.)

Soon it was time for little Anthony to learn to drink out of a cup. Grandma was

In dePaola's original handwritten draft, baby Anthony falls asleep at lunch after his christening. Grandma observes that he isn't paying attention.

On Anthony's first birthday there was a feast of all feasts. In the shade of the olive grove, the family and friends sat at tables piled high with food . Papa stood to give a birthday greeting.

"Sit quietly, my son, and listen to Papa," Mama whispered to Anthony. Papa began to speak, but before he had even said *Felice Compleanno* " "Happy Birthday," there was a loud crash. Everyone looked around and saw Anthony covered in cake.

"Hmmmm," Nonna said. "Little Anthony may be a bit of trouble."

Little Anthony began to grow.

"He's going to be a big boy," Nonna said. "He takes after my side of the family."

Soon it was time for Anthony to learn to drink out of a cup. Nonna was going to teach him.

"Hold your cup in both hands." Anthony did.     " Lift it up " And Anthony did.

"Now drink." Just then a bird sang.

"He doesn't pay attention," Nonna said. "That's the trouble."

And Nonna was right.

addition

Every year Anthony grew taller. Soon he was big enough to help on the farm.

"Here's a basket, Anthony. Go to the garden and pick the lettuce the way I showed you. Then bring it to me in the kitchen," Mama told him.

Anthony did.

2

In a revised version, dePaola and his editor Frith decide that something more momentous needs to happen to show Anthony's lack of attention. The christening lunch is changed to a first birthday party, where he upsets cake all over himself. Grandma has become "Nonna."

rough drafts, printing proofs, and final copy to be reproduced here permits a glimpse of the creativity, the work, the care, the detail, the time, and the love that go into just one of his books.

*Big Anthony, His Story* takes the reader from the time Big Anthony is born in northern Italy to the day he meets Strega Nona in Calabria in the south and becomes her lovable but oafish assistant.

From the day he was born, Big Anthony never paid attention. "Hmmm," Nonna Graziella said. "Little Anthony may be a bit of trouble." In two episodes early in the story, reproduced below, little Anthony upsets his cake on his first birthday, and learns to drink from a cup, only to have a singing bird distract him, causing him to spill milk all over himself.

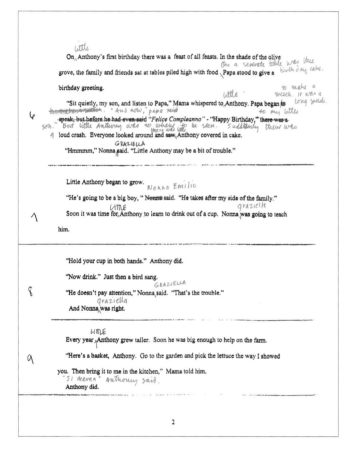

"Sit quietly, my son, and listen to Papa," Mama whispered to little Anthony. Papa began to make a speech. It was a long speech. "And now," Papa said, "Felice Compleanno—Happy Birthday—to my little son." But little Anthony was no where to be seen. Suddenly there was a loud crash. Everyone looked around, and there was little Anthony, covered in cake.

"Hmmm," Nonna Graziella said. "Little Anthony may be a bit of trouble."

Little Anthony began to grow.

"He's going to be a big boy," Nonno Emilio said. "He takes after my side of the family."

Soon it was time for little Anthony to learn to drink out of a cup. Nonna Graziella was going to teach him.

"Hold your cup in both hands." Anthony did.

"Lift it up." And Anthony did.

"Now drink." Just then a bird sang.

"He doesn't pay attention," Nonna Graziella said. "That's the trouble." And Nonna Graziella was right.

Every year little Anthony grew taller. Soon he was big enough to help on the farm.

"Here's a basket, Anthony. Go to the garden and pick the lettuce the way I showed you. Then bring it to me in the kitchen," Mama told him.

"Si, Mama," Anthony said.

Anthony did.

"Oh, Anthony!" Mama said.

In the final version, Anthony has changed back to "little Anthony" and Nonna has become "Nonna Graziella." To allow for the "turn of page" visual surprise, which dePaola uses throughout the book, the birthday episode is rewritten again.

The final text is set in galleys.

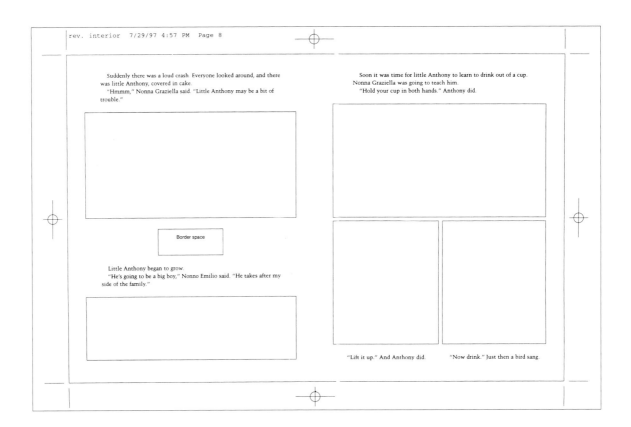

Suddenly there was a loud crash. Everyone looked around, and there was little Anthony, covered in cake.

"Hmmm," Nonna Graziella said. "Little Anthony may be a bit of trouble."

Border space

Little Anthony began to grow.

"He's going to be a big boy," Nonno Emilio said. "He takes after my side of the family."

Soon it was time for little Anthony to learn to drink out of a cup. Nonna Graziella was going to teach him.

"Hold your cup in both hands." Anthony did.

"Lift it up." And Anthony did.          "Now drink." Just then a bird sang.

In consultation with dePaola, the designer prepares a grid for the illustrations.

Using the grid, dePaola creates his sketches.

The story art is finished. Rabbits, still in sketches, serve as a decorative transition between the episodes.

A laser printout instructs the printer on the art and type placement—FPO indicates "For Position Only."
Birds now replace the rabbits in this completed image, making the decorative transition elements
a part of the spirit of the story—in this case the bird that distracts little Anthony.

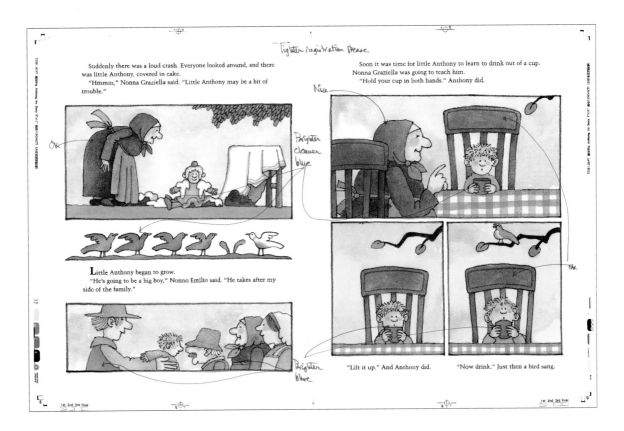

These first proofs from the printer permit the checking of page size, position of art and type, and color. Corrections to color are marked directly on the proof.

The double-page spread as it appears in the printed book.

DePaola's rough sketch, LEFT, becomes his final jacket image, BELOW. Haystacks, a house, and hills round out the background; meanwhile, Big Anthony imperturbably poses in a loving spoof of the Mona Lisa.

*"Bravissimo, mio caro Tomie!"* As ebullient as ever,
Strega Nona waves greetings to her fans at the World Financial Center in 1993.

# DePaola Off Page

Over the years, dePaola has garnered a legion of fans. As a result, his characters, called "pillow people" by some children, have found themselves from time to time in places far from the printed page. Beguiled retailers, astutely recognizing sales potential, continually request permission to incorporate his characters and design motifs into their products.

One of the first was Neiman-Marcus,[1] who asked dePaola to design its Christmas catalog cover and shopping bag. His creations, based on his elaborate pop-up book *Giorgio's Village,* portray children of the Renaissance celebrating the holiday festival. Pleased, the company issued limited-edition Christmas cards, paper napkins, and cocktail glasses (the latter are now collector's items), and offered the book for sale in its stores and catalog. "I got calls from people I hadn't heard from in years," dePaola says, "but the exposure was great. It reached almost two million people. It's like an actor on Broadway suddenly being on a television program."[2]

The Dayton department stores in Minneapolis zeroed in on dePaola's talent, inviting him to create a design for "A Children's Garden of Verses, Songs, Games...and Other Things," their Dayton's-Bachman's Annual Flower Show.[3] "After coming up with the theme," dePaola says, "I was given the number of square feet to work with, and then, in conjunction with Bachman florists, I devised a ground plan that included designating areas for the different kinds of flowers and deciding where the

various structures and paths would go. The most crucial—and most fun—was the color design, thinking about the hues of various flowers and then coordinating their placement. It was my first experience in landscape design—and it was great."

The interplay of light and color across animals, water, and buildings displays the care dePaola brought to the Dayton's-Bachman's Annual Flower Show in 1989.

Following on the Neiman-Marcus success, assistant Bob Hechtel sent a copy of *The Popcorn Book* to The Popcorn Factory in Lake Forest, Illinois.[4] "It seemed," he said, "a natural tie-in, since Tomie counts popcorn as one of his 'most favorite foods' and since *The Popcorn Book* has had continuing appeal over the years." The company marketed popcorn in cans decorated with scenes adapted from *The Night Before Christmas*, and quickly found it had a popular seller. Later, they asked dePaola to adapt vignettes from *An Early American Christmas* and *Country Angel Christmas* (available through the catalog) for its popular tin containers. These, too, quickly became in demand around the country, especially when featured on the cover of the company's catalog.

DePaola motifs dance around popcorn tins designed for The Popcorn Factory in Lake Forest, Illinois.

An even bigger effort by a Minnesota-based company, Midwest of Cannon Falls,[5] resulted in a 100-item line of Christmas products made from resin, tin, wood, or fabric. Molded ornaments and such giftware items as bookends, candelabras, Nativity sets, and painted child-size tables and chairs—all based on characters from dePaola's *Country Angel Christmas* and other Christmas books—now grace Christmas-decorated homes across the country. Although dePaola didn't create the three-dimensional objects himself, he closely consulted with the twenty-five company artists and approved all the final work; his signature is reproduced on nearly every piece. One year, dePaola devoted one of the several Christmas trees in his home to these ornaments—a menagerie that includes white birds, children with harps and mixing bowls, multicultural angels, winged dogs that bear a strong resemblance to his Welsh terriers, and a variety of gaily dressed Santas. To help promote the endeavor, he hopscotched across the country on a whirlwind forty-city tour, making several appearances at Marshall Field's department stores in Chicago. "It was," dePaola remembers, "exhausting."

The following year, Midwest of Cannon Falls concentrated on the Strega Nona and Big Anthony characters, issuing ornaments, needlepoint pillows, and other three-dimensional objects. Unfortunately, these charming lagniappes are no longer available; Midwest has discontinued the line.

DePaola's "Whitebird" is the inspiration for this handsome Christmas tree topper for Midwest of Cannon Falls.

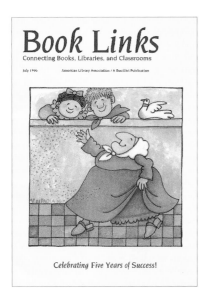

DePaola designed this original piece of art to help *Book Links* celebrate its fifth anniversary.

In response to other requests, dePaola has created covers for *Book Links, Cricket,* and *Baby Bug* magazines and for Lands' End Kids catalogs, has accommodated *Country Home* magazine's request for a Christmas-time photo essay on his home, and has designed many reading promotional endeavors across the country.[6]

DePaola's childhood claims—that he would one day write stories and draw pictures for children and be on the stage—have been melded into what has been a long and lasting connection with the Children's Theatre Company in Minneapolis,[7] a liaison that began in 1981. Artistic director John Clark Donahue, browsing through a book display at the Walker Art Center, came upon a copy of *The Clown of God.* Donahue told *Minneapolis Star* interviewer Peter Vaughan, "From the moment I saw the book, I knew we had to put it on here."[8] He got his wish and a month-long visit from dePaola, who became an integral part of the production from serving as design consultant to the costume and set department to providing illustrations for the program. DePaola commented that he and Donahue worked well together because "we are both concerned with the same commodity: the imagination of children."[9] The show sold out; when it opened on February 28, 1981,

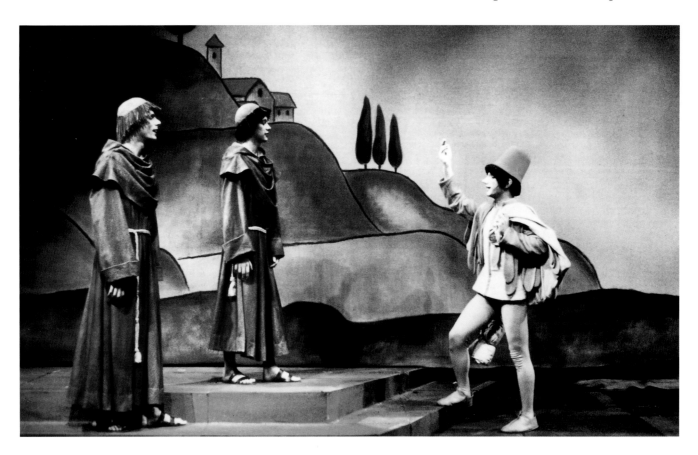

Giovanni at center stage in this scene from the Children's Theatre Company production of *The Clown of God.*

*Minneapolis Tribune* reviewer Mike Steele called it a "Renaissance painting in motion."[10] Its success instigated repeat performances in following years as well as stagings of *Strega Nona* and *Tomie dePaola's Mother Goose.*

A stage appearance of another kind cast dePaola in the role of narrator for two New Hampshire Philharmonic Orchestra concerts. On the first occasion, he read *The Mysterious Giant of Barletta* and *Days of the Blackbird* to the music of the *William Tell* Overture and of Respighi's *The Birds* and Vivaldi's *Four Seasons,* respectively. The second time, he read *The Clown of God* to the accompaniment of Chabrier's *Suite Pastorale,* and *The Legend of the Poinsettia* to that of Copeland's *Appalachian Spring* and Ravel's *Mother Goose Suite.*[11]

The stage, however, has not been the only platform for dePaola's performances. Public television's *Barney and Friends* invited him twice to draw and tell stories to the eighteen million two- to four-year-olds that watch the show daily.[12] "To them," dePaola says, "I live in the television set!"[13] The first children's artist-author to be on the show, he made a third appearance, this time with sister Maureen, following the publication of *The Baby Sister.*

Again on public television but in another venue—*Ciao Italia* hosted by Mary Ann Esposito—the artist used his hands not to draw pictures but to beat, cut, chop, and stir as he worked alongside this noted Italian gourmet cook.[14] In four shows to date, the duo has whipped up such sumptuous Italian dishes as Easter breads, panetone, Befana cake, and summer dishes on the grill. After his first stint on Esposito's show, which dePaola said "was a thrill," and then illustrating her book *Celebrations, Italian Style,* they agreed to find time for more joint appearances. Their pleasure in food and their camaraderie shines through the screen.

Another thrill, and one he is most proud of, was creating an original poster for Food Research and Action Center (FRAC), an organization he has long supported. At FRAC's twenty-fifth anniversary dinner, held in Washington D.C., on June 7, 1995, dePaola presented a signed, numbered, and framed copy of the poster to First Lady Hillary Clinton. Her response: "Oh, Tomie, I just love you!"[15]

Perhaps one of the most unusual places where dePaola's characters have turned up is in Guy Kawasaki's adult business bestseller *How to Drive Your Competition Crazy.*[16] In a chapter entitled "Make the Competition into a Friend," he reproduces *The Knight and the Dragon* in its entirety (albeit in black and white). The story, which ends with the not-so-fierce knight and the sheepish-looking dragon going into the barbecue business together, nicely demonstrates Kawasaki's point about making your

Two good friends share a hug.

DePaola at the White House.

enemy a friend. Kawasaki also notes, "I derive three benefits: First, I get to use a terrific story by a topnotch children's author; second, his work adds an unusual graphic element to a 'business book'; and third, I don't have to write a chapter."

The two feisty enemies-turned-friends also found their story fully reproduced in *Crayola Kids* magazine,[17] along with photos and a question-and-answer session with dePaola, which focused on children's writing efforts. The feature, which invited children to make a drawing about the knight and the dragon and to create a self-portrait as an artist in a studio and send it to dePaola, generated thousands of letters, which he answered with a special mailing.

And the list goes on. For a 1998 reading initiative, Read Across America, sponsored by the National Education Association, dePaola provided an amusing yet meaningful logo for the Certificate of Participation—a drawing of the Statue of Liberty, down off her pedestal, torch at her side, reading to children.[18] DePaola's own characters have found themselves on a poster for the 1983 Children's Book Week celebration[19] (in a harlequin theme); as soft dolls (She-Who-Is-Alone, Strega Nona, and Maggie's Monster) for MerryMakers[20]; on rubber stamps (Strega Nona, Big Anthony, Charlie) for Kidstamps[21]; as subjects of an Advent calendar and a giant floor puzzle[22]; and decorating tote bags and T-shirts by the dozen. In fact, solicitations for use of dePaola's drawings, for exhibiting his art, for copies of signed books, for creating posters and T-shirts, and for putting his books onto CD-ROMs[23] have become so overwhelming that he has had to hire a cadre of people to help him. In addition to his assistant, Bob Hechtel, Sherry Litwack[24] manages the sale of his original artwork and various sideline items through her own Hollyhock Press; Val Hornburg,[25] a teacher in Oregon, has put together a resource manual for using dePaola's books in the classroom; a publicity assistant at Putnam coordinates his speaking schedule; sister Maureen serves as bookkeeper; and a mail handler goes through more than 100,000 letters yearly.

The children's letters are a particular concern for the artist. While he continues to answer some personally, he reluctantly hired an assistant in order to keep current. "Otherwise," he says, "I would never get any books written or illustrated." Wanting children to know that he appreciates their letters, he devises an original bookmark each year that is sent only to the letter writers, along with a handwritten, preprinted letter.

As original exhibitions of children's illustrations grew in popularity in the late 1980s, requests to include dePaola's work in shows or to mount ones featuring only his art also escalated. Several very special (to

MerryMakers version of She-Who-Is-Alone from *The Legend of the Bluebonnet.*

him) exhibits resulted. Ronne Hartfield, director of museum education at the Art Institute of Chicago, exhibited dePaola's artwork at the illustrators' gallery in 1992.[26] More than twenty pieces of dePaola's work were displayed, and the artist made an appearance to open the show.

The Cedar Rapids Museum of Art[27] mounted two shows. *The Art of the Heart Man*, so named for obvious reasons, traveled extensively as did the celebration of the artist's sixtieth birthday—*Tomie Turns 60! New Art for Children by Tomie dePaola*. The latter, curated by Sherry Litwack, proved to be one of the museum's most popular shows. When

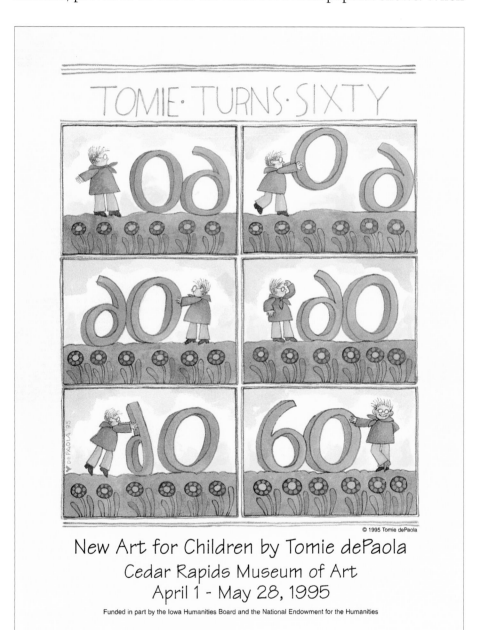

© 1995 Tomie dePaola

New Art for Children by Tomie dePaola
Cedar Rapids Museum of Art
April 1 - May 28, 1995

Funded in part by the Iowa Humanities Board and the National Endowment for the Humanities

DePaola re-creates the "chicken feet" episode from *Tom*.

it traveled to (among other places) the Rock County Historical Society Museum in Janesville, Wisconsin, public relations director Jane Kerr said that the eighty-some pieces attracted "thousands of children (and adults) who jubilantly explored dePaola's work through story hours, music, activities, food, games, and especially his original art."[28]

It is not surprising that thousands of children trooped through a museum to view dePaola's work. In addition to the mountain of letters he receives, dePaola gets what to him is an amazing number of requests (nearly a thousand a year) to speak at schools, universities, conferences, and art museums. "It's hard to say no," dePaola comments, "and sometimes I don't!"

Two Portland, Oregon, booksellers[29] lured dePaola to the Northwest with plans for programs, autographing parties, and parades. He was not disappointed: Four hundred children dressed as characters from his books cavorted down Main Street to the delight of fans who lined the way. In California, a librarian dreamed up a similar week-plus-long festivity.[30] In both cases, dePaola's publishers as well as local public and school libraries and television and radio stations helped put the "Tomie Show" on the road. He also said yes to the Children's Book Council

Children, some as costumed characters from his books, accompany the author down the main street in New London, New Hampshire.

of Australia's invitation to go down under in 1998 as the keynote speaker for its biannual conference, combining the trip with a 'round-the-world vacation.[31] DePaola's visits to Australia whetted his interest in supporting a show entitled *Down Under & Over Here*, featuring artwork from thirty-two prominent American and twenty-two prominent Australian illustrators that will tour in the U. S. A. from 1998 through the year 2000.[32]

Towns and villages near his home in New England frequently ask dePaola to provide programs for teachers, librarians, and parents; give radio, television, and newspaper interviews; and to read his stories to children, and dePaola has been generous to the "hometown" crowd.

Christmas comes to New London each year in the guise of this Santa's Cottage, courtesy of dePaola.

For instance, dePaola is heavily involved in New London's Christmas observances. He designed a nontraditional Santa Claus outfit (red-and-black plaid with green plaid leggings). "After all," dePaola says chuckling, "Santa has to save his *best* costume for Christmas Eve, doesn't he?"[33] Then, each December the New London information booth is turned into Santa's Cottage, decorated with three-foot wooden figures that he designed and that were constructed and painted by art students at Colby-Sawyer College. A large mailbox on-site invites children to mail their Santa letters. On the first Friday night of December, a Santa parade heads down Main Street, ending at the cottage; dePaola is almost always in attendance.[34] Those unable to travel to New Hampshire for this festivity can see a version of it in dePaola's *Country Angel Christmas,* where his illustrations are the prototypes for Santa's costume and for the figures and decorations on and around Santa's Cottage.

169

New London's children's librarian Timmie Poh helps the hometown artist-author dedicate The Tomie dePaola Room, RIGHT; and FAR RIGHT, a summer reading program.

New London has responded to dePaola's continuous generosity by dedicating the children's room in the Tracy Memorial Library to him,[35] while the Richards Free Library[36] in Newport, New Hampshire set up a Tomie dePaola Reading Room. New London's Tomie dePaola Room, decorated with prints and original drawings, features a large bookcase containing duplicate volumes from dePaola's own archival collection. There, among his familiar characters, he conducts summer reading programs, sometimes delighting children with new stories he has written and encouraging them to participate as he reads aloud.

His hometown of Meriden, Connecticut, also has honored the artist. In 1985, coinciding with the publication of *Tomie dePaola's Mother Goose*, which dePaola dedicated to "all my friends in my old hometown," Meriden held a three-day "Welcome Home Tomie" celebration that included a parade (dePaola was grand marshal) with costumed characters from his books, a "Story and Drawing Hour with Tomie" for the children, and a "Strega Nona Magical Spaghetti Dinner;" it concluded with dePaola being inducted into the Meriden Hall of Fame.[37] A reprise occurred in 1993, when the artist provided a one-man dramatic reading of *Tom*, set in Meriden and nearby Wallingford, and presided over the "Positively Stupendous Strega Nona Pasta Dinner" put on by both libraries.[38]

To help compensate for dePaola's inability to be everywhere, Whitebird, Inc. produced a video, *A Visit with Tomie dePaola*, in 1996.[39]

Its success spurred a second filming during a live presentation in Manchester, New Hamphire. *Tomie dePaola, Live in Concert* finds the artist-author drawing, telling stories, and entertaining a large roomful of families. The first video is more personal in tone, and conversational: The camera deftly accompanies the artist on a tour of his home and studio and looks over his shoulder as he works on one of his illustrations.

One of the surprises in the *A Visit with Tomie dePaola* video may well be the introduction to dePaola's non-book art. While in his beginning years as an artist he painted large, liturgical pieces, he stopped doing that to fulfill his many book obligations. Recently, dePaola has returned to this venue, finding, he says, satisfaction in both much smaller and much larger canvases and in lighter and much heavier palettes as a change of pace from his illustration work.

*"The Being of God is the beauty of all there is"*—Self portrait
oil on canvas
36" x 29 3/4"
1956

# DePaola's Non-Book Art

The bins full of art in his barn loft, the small still-life paintings that hang on his walls, the shadow boxes containing bits of realia that perch in alcoves, and the files brimming with costume and scenery sketches offer another side to dePaola's artistic inclinations. In his early career, he was one of a handful of people working in contemporary liturgical art, and his talents were in great demand. He also has designed fabric for a weaving studio, made vestments for the chapel on the Île de France, created the architectural drawings for his present studio, and sculpted masks used in the stage production of *The Clown of God*.

"In recent years," dePaola says, "in order to keep my picture-book art fresh, I've been making pencil and watercolor drawings and large splashy paintings on paper. One of the best parts," he says with a grin, "is getting to use bigger brushes."[1] Beginning in 1998, some of these works became available to the public through an association with Beacon Fine Arts, who began producing fine art serigraphs of some of dePaola's folk art.[2] DePaola continues, in more serious reflection: "I find it very freeing, in a sense. In my picture books, I'm always watching to see that the image is appropriate to the story and to the subject matter, and I'm always trying to second-guess what my editor or art director might be looking for. When I do these other things, I do them just for myself. And yet my heart will always be thoroughly grounded in my books for children."

*Watermelon*
acrylic on paper
11" x 12"
1991

On the following pages, a highly selective "gallery tour" gives a glimpse of, as a recent exhibit at Colby-Sawyer College was aptly entitled, *Tomie dePaola's Other Side.*[3]

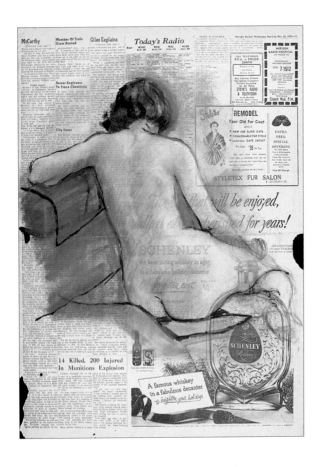

*Life Study, Pratt Institute*
22 3/4" x 16 1/2"
pastel and ink on newspaper
circa 1953

*Figure Study, Pratt Institute*
ink and colored pastels on paper
24" x 19 1/4"
circa 1952-1956

*Crowd Scene Assignment*
*Pratt Institute*
tempera on illustration board
16″ x 19″
circa 1952-1956

*Maureen*
oil on canvas
22″ x 30″
1954

175

*Geraniums*
oil on canvas
18″ x 23 3/4″
1955

*Woman with Orange*
casein on illustration board
20″ x 8 1/2″
1956

176

*Self portrait*
oil on canvas
19" x 29"
1954

*The Good Shepherd*
oil on canvas
36″ x 24″
1956

*Cousin Kitty*
oil on canvas
16 1/4″ x 16 1/4″
1966

*Italian Grandparents: Concetta and Antonio*
oil on canvas
18″ x 24″
1966

*FEP*
oil on canvas
36″ x 36″
1966

*Still Life*
oil on canvas
10″ x 14 1/2″
1977

*Cousin Rachel*
oil on canvas
31″ x 30″
1966

*Angel*
acrylic on canvas
30″ x 20″
1986

*Angel on a Pear for Bob—*
*Christmas 1994*
acrylic on paper
7 1/2" x 5 1/2"
1994

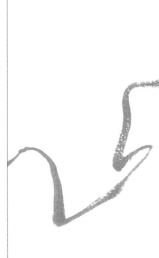

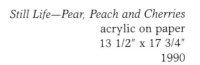

*Still Life—Pear, Peach and Cherries*
acrylic on paper
13 1/2" x 17 3/4"
1990

*Blue Chair*
acrylic on paper
22″ x 30″
1989

183

*Frida's Table*
acrylic on canvas
5′ x 4′
1995

*Watermelon Slice, Pears & Kelly's Horse*
acrylic on canvas
18″ x 24″
1996

*Frida's Kitchen*
acrylic and collage on paper
22″ x 30″
1995

*The Cherry Thief*
acrylic on canvas
4′ x 5′
1998

# A Visit from an Old Professor
*By Roger Crossgrove*

It was a clear spring day when I visited Tomie recently in his New London home and studio. The flowers and lawns and the views from the gazebo and swimming pool echoed the colors and compositional base that I was familiar with through his picture books. After all, I have been looking at, reading to my children and grandchildren, and collecting his books for more than thirty years.

Inside, I was treated to a visual feast of images—a watercolor of a young man with a lamb on his shoulder, a scene of the Virgin of Guadalupe, an angel on a pear, and a mother and child and a moon. On our way to view slides of his past work (our project for the day), I passed several rows of large acrylic paintings, which I later learned were being photographed and documented for an upcoming exhibition at The Cove Gallery in Wellfleet, Massachusetts. There was a haunting landscape with three trees, a house, and a foreground of fields; a "cherry thief"—a blackbird with a "Who me?" look in his eye and stance; a long bench with a purple-and-green striped seat cover, and then, a huge orange against a blue field, stripped of all nonessentials. I was stopped by the orange, puzzled. It stirred a memory I couldn't quite catch. "Revenge?" The word came and went, surely without connection here.

I spent the afternoon looking at hundreds of images. Tomie (or his mother!) had saved everything—from early childhood drawings through stacks of work from his Pratt Institute days to last week's watercolor of a still life with watermelon. The boxes of Pratt work offer a short, select record of the educational program for training artist-illustrators: figure drawings from Mr. Albert's class, two- and three-dimensional design projects from Mr. Whiteman's class, a pastel and charcoal drawing of Anita Lobel as a Spanish dancer from Mr. Bove's class, a moon juggler, the girls of the Kit Kat Klub with mesh stockings, garters, and hands on hips, a picture of jaunty seductiveness. Here was early evidence of Tomie's inborn ability to see and re-present the telling gesture in line, color, shape, and texture to find just the right image to tell the story.

And then there was the painting of the apples—one of my "Fall Scenes" still-life projects for Sophomore Painting, required of all majors in the illustration program. Tomie's (breakthrough) solution was to make a very big painting some sixty inches long of red apples; it was by far the largest in the class.

When it got to be 6:30 that evening, Tomie left Bob (his assistant) and me and went to his "chef's heaven" kitchen to prepare dinner. Later, we joined him—sitting on stools in the kitchen, a glass of Rockford Basket Press Shiraz in hand—while Tomie chopped, stirred, turned, tossed, and tasted. When he announced that dinner was ready, we moved to the dining room, ablaze with candles on the table, on the sideboard, in the candelabra overhead, and in the wall sconces. More wine for toasting each other's contributions to the slide documentation project at hand and its future as well as to the dinner—presented picture perfect—and, then of course, to the inevitable good old days when we were at Pratt.

We told stories and interrupted each other with tales about classmates long forgotten as well as those who are now familiar names in libraries, bookstores, museums, galleries, schools, and homes around the world: Susan Jeffers, Chuck Mikolaycak, Arnold and Anita Lobel, John Schoenherr, Gerald McDermott, Cyndy Szekeres—the list went on. Suddenly, it was Brooklyn in the 1950s: rows of brownstones, the Myrtle Avenue El, Fort Greene Park, the cannon near the library in the little Pratt Institute Park. We talked about the teachers at Pratt and their classes, the favorites and the ones less so.

As Tomie began telling Bob (had he heard this before?) about his first painting in my sophomore class, I recalled my earlier elusive memory upon seeing that orange and began to sense that something was about to reveal itself. Tomie set the stage with a grandiose description of the classroom—the easels, stools, and painting tables that had been arranged for each student in semi-circles around several shadow boxes, each containing a still life I had set up for that day. He recalled his excitement about his first painting in his first painting class. And what did his shadow box contain? A chunk of black coal and a white hard-cooked egg, beautifully lighted to define the various planes and tonal values as well as the textures and surfaces of the two objects. At least, that's how I saw it. I had been pleased with this exercise in the basics. As for Tomie? I certainly don't remember the classroom mood or any comments made at the time, but it's probably just as well.

Tomie's still-life apples would come later and his grade would move from the generic C to an A by the end of the term. But that day, I'd given him an egg and a lump of coal. And now on this day, looking at that huge glowing orange, I'd thought "revenge" and, though I didn't ask him, it was—the Revenge of the Egg! Those long years back, a small, colorless object had sat motionless and cold against an even colder, more motionless piece of coal. Today, I'd been knocked out by a vibrant orange (egg?) bigger than life, bright, round, ripe, and full. I call that sweet revenge. What a marvelous moment, just one of the many in a long-standing friendship with this wonderful man whose work will be admired and loved for generations to come.[4]

*Big Orange*
acrylic on canvas
3' x 3'
1998

# Appendix

## Notes and References

The quotations and much of the information in this book were taken from formal interviews with Tomie dePaola in November 1996 and in May and December 1997, and from casual conversations, telephone calls, and notes made during various dePaola speeches over the last twenty years. The statistics on books, mail, and other data were provided by Bob Hechtel.

### INTRODUCTION

1. Nancy Cobb, "Tomie's Gift," *Northeast: The Hartford Courant Sunday Magazine,* December 25, 1994.

### A LIFE

1. Information about Tomie dePaola can be found on the World Wide Web at http://www.bingley.com

2. *Something about the Author: Autobiographical Series.* Detroit: Gale Research, 1993, 15: 87.

3. *Something about the Author: Autobiographical Series.* 15: 92.

4. *Southern Vermont Valley News,* October 24, 1980.

5. *Something about the Author: Autobiographical Series.* 15: 96.

6. Florence Nesci, a friend of the dePaola family, lived in nearby Yalesville, Connecticut.

7. Frances (Franny) McLaughlin-Gill and Kathryn (Fuffy) Abbe were pictured (holding cards #10 and #15) in Guy Trebay's article "All Together Now," which featured top contemporary women photographers in New York. *New York,* November 4, 1996, p. 45.

8. Anita Lobel received a 1980 Caldecott Honor designation for *On Market Street* (Greenwillow), written by Arnold Lobel; Arnold Lobel won the 1981 Caldecott Medal for *Fables* (Harper); John Schoenherr won the 1988 Caldecott Medal for *Owl Moon* (Philomel), written by Jane Yolen; and Ted Lewin received a 1994 Caldecott Honor for *Peppe the Lamplighter* (Lothrop), written by Elisa Bartone.

9. Ruth Krauss, *A Hole Is to Dig: A First Book of First Definitions,* illustrated by Maurice Sendak. New York: Harper, 1952.

10. Alice and Martin Provensen wrote and illustrated titles such as *The Year at Maple Hill Farm* (Atheneum) and *A Peaceable Kingdom: The Shaker Abecedarius* (Viking), and were awarded the 1984 Caldecott Medal for *The Glorious Flight: Across the Channel with Louis Blériot* (Viking).

11. Sequence illustration is a technique dePaola often uses to show several action events with the same characters on the same page. Examples can be found in *"Charlie Needs a Cloak"* and *Mary Had a Little Lamb.*

12. French expressionist Georges Rouault (1871-1958) is best known for his mythological and religious canvases.

13. Works by Ben Shahn (1898-1969) hang in the Museum of Modern Art in New York City.

14. The Skowhegan School of Painting and Sculpture is located in Skowhegan, Maine.

15. DePaola quoted Shahn during an interview on *Home Matters*, which aired on The Discovery Channel October 28 and December 12, 1997.

16. Leo Lionni, *Between Worlds: The Autobiography of Leo Lionni.* New York: Knopf, 1997.

17. Alastair Reid, *Ounce, Dice, Trice,* illustrated by Ben Shahn. Boston: Little, Brown, 1958.

18. Mother Placid resides at the Abbey of Regina Laudis, Bethlehem, Connecticut.

19. The documentary, "The Search for the *Andrea Doria*," was televised on A&E.

20. DePaola had used "Thomas dePaola" on his traveler's checks to match the signature on his passport.

21. Weston Priory, in Weston, Vermont, is a Benedictine monastery.

22. DePaola married Monique Chéret in 1959; they divorced in 1961.

23. For the Glastonbury Monastery, Hingham, Massachusetts, dePaola designed a crucifix, which was modeled and cast in bronze; painted a second crucifix on wood; painted stations of the cross on the chapel walls; painted a mural of St. Benedict on a chapel wall; lettered the entryway; and painted three murals in the refectory.

24. The Dominican Retreat House Center for Renewal, 1945 Union Street, Schenectady, New York 12309, is the chapel where dePaola created ten-foot-high figures for an expansive mural; it was his first big commission. The mural depicting female saints important to the Dominican order of sisters is the focal point of the chapel. The center's administrator, Jeanne Qualters, says that "teachers familiar with dePaola's books recognize his work when they visit." Karen Bjornland, "Book Signings Planned," *The Daily Gazette* (Schenectady), November 3, 1997.

25. Chronology of dePaola's teaching career

    1962-1963: Instructor of Art, Newton College of the Sacred Heart, Newton, Massachusetts

    1963-1966: Assistant Professor of Art, Newton College of the Sacred Heart, Newton, Massachusetts

    1967-1970: Assistant Professor of Art, Lone Mountain College, San Francisco (then called San Francisco College for Women), California

    1972-1973: Instructor of Art, Chamberlayne Junior College, Boston, Massachusetts

    1973-1976: Associate Professor, Designer, Technical Director in Speech and Theater, Colby-Sawyer College, New London, New Hampshire

    1976-1978: Associate Professor of Art, New England College, Henniker, New Hampshire

    1978-1979: Artist-in-Residence, New England College, Henniker, New Hampshire

26. Tomie dePaola, "A Talent Takes Wing," *Guideposts,* April 1990.

27. Mary Zeman, "His Vocation Is Telling Stories with Words and Images," *Books & Religion,* March/April 1987.

28. Home liturgies were popular in the 1960s among those pulling away from organized religion yet still wanting worship in their lives.

29. "White Bird" was composed in 1967 by David LaFlamme, the leader of the rock group It's A Beautiful Day.

30. Candace Ord Manroe, "Tomie's Christmas Story," *Country Home,* December 1992.

31. Midwest of Cannon Falls, one of the country's leading giftware companies, is based in Cannon Falls, Minnesota.

32. Tomie dePaola, "Christmas is when the invisible becomes visible," Voices of New England, *The Boston Sunday Globe,* December 24, 1995.

33. The Botolph Group, Cambridge and Boston, owned and operated by Celia Hubbard, specialized in contemporary liturgical art.

34. Florence Alexander lived in New York City and was dePaola's artist representative from 1964 until she died in 1993.

35. *Something about the Author: Autobiographical Series.* 15: 100.

36. The physical science series was called Science Is What and Why.

## AUTOBIOGRAPHICAL TALES

1. Ellen Roberts, *The Children's Picture Book: How to Write It, How to Sell It.* New York: Writer's Digest, 1981.

2. Margaret Frith has worked with dePaola since 1964.

3. Conversation with dePaola's Putnam editor Margaret Frith, April 1997.

4. Tommy (and Tomie) called his paternal grandmother Nana Fall-River because she lived in Fall River, Massachusetts.

5. Aunt Nell, a favorite of dePaola's, was his mother's aunt.

6. Quote from back flap of *Flicks*. The back jacket's illustration depicts a billboard reading "Holiday Flicks to Come"; that suggested sequel, however, never materialized.

7. Charles Massey, a New York theatrical manager and a friend of dePaola's, was responsible for supplying new cast members to *A Chorus Line* in its early years on Broadway.

8. Library of Congress Cataloging-in-Publication Data (CIP) lists "Artists—Fiction" and "Individuality—Fiction" as subject headings on the copyright page.

## RELIGIOUS BOOKS

1. Joseph of Copertino (some sources list Cupertino) became a saint in 1767 and patron saint of aviators in the twentieth century; his feast day is September 18.

2. Pura Belpré, a well-known storyteller, was honored in 1996 by an award in her name. Administered by the American Library Association and REFORMA, the award was created to honor Latino writers and illustrators whose work best portrays, affirms, and celebrates the Latino cultural experience in the work of literature for youth.

3. Russell Freedman, *Holiday House: The First Fifty Years.* New York: Holiday House, 1985.

4. F. R. Webber, *Church Symbolism: An Explanation of the More Important Symbols of the Old and New Testament, the Primitive, the Mediaeval and the Modern Church.* Cleveland: J. H. Hansen, 2nd ed. rev. 1938.

5. St. Francis was born in 1182; his eight hundredth birth anniversary inspired numerous celebrations around the world.

6. Giotto (1267-1337), *St. Francis Preaching to the Birds,* Upper Basilica of San Francesco, San Francesco, Assisi.

7. Barbara Cooney, *The Little Juggler.* New York: Hastings House, 1961.

8. Vittore Carpaccio (1450-1522), *Miracle of the Relic of the True Cross,* Gallerie dell'Accademe, Venice, Italy.

## CHRISTMAS STORIES

1. Patricia Bunning Stevens, *Merry Christmas: A History of the Holiday.* New York: Macmillan, 1979.

2. Washington Irving, *Diedrich Knickerbocker's History of New York from the Beginning of the World to the End of the Dutch Dynasty.* New York: Inskeep & Bradford, 1809.

3. Clement C. Moore, *The Night Before Christmas,* illustrated by Grandma Moses. New York: Random House, Reissue, 1976.

## FOLKTALES

1. Piero Canuto is owner/chef of La Meridiana Restaurant in Wilmot Flat, New Hampshire. DePaola, unsuccessful in his search to find a written version of the legend, concluded that it was a bit of oral lore; Canuto confirmed that by saying he remembered hearing the legend as a child from his teacher.

2. Linda Morley was a teacher of folklore at New England College.

3. DePaola studied photographs of the paintings on Dinkelsbühl's town hall when illustrating the book.

4. Margaret Looper, a reading consultant in Huntsville, Texas, urged dePaola to tell and illustrate the tale about the Texas bluebonnet and sent him background information on the Comanche People.

5. DePaola credits Pat Henry, a reading teacher in Wyoming; Carolyn Sullivan from Austin, Texas; and Ruth D. Isely, author of *Texas Wildflowers, Stories and Legends,* as instrumental in bringing this Plains tale to fruition. Little Gopher, however, is his own invention.

6. Strega Nona was conceived on dePaola's doodle pad while at a faculty meeting at Colby-Sawyer College in 1974.

## STREGA NONA

1. The Children's Theatre Company, Minneapolis, Minnesota, first presented *Strega Nona* in 1986. The musical, an adaptation based on *Strega Nona, Big Anthony and the Magic Ring,* and *Strega Nona's Magic Lessons,* has been revived several times and has toured in the Midwest to great reviews.

2. The Strega Nona doll is produced by MerryMakers, Inc.; Strega Nona wall hangings are available from Demco, Inc., Madison, Wisconsin; Strega Nona pillows and ornaments are by Midwest of Cannon Falls; Strega Nona tote bags are by Kidstamps; the Strega Nona balloon appeared at Universal Studios, Orlando, September 10, 1996, and at the World Financial Center Children's Book and Activity Fair, in association with Rizzoli Bookstores, on November 12-14, 1993, in New York City.

3. *Strega Nona,* published by Prentice-Hall in 1975, edited by Ellen Roberts, was named an Honor Book by the 1976 Newbery/Caldecott Committee, chaired by Zena Sutherland. The medal that year was awarded to Leo and Diane Dillon for *Why Mosquitoes Buzz in People's Ears* (Dial).

4. Grandma Concetta, Strega Nona's grandmother, is the name of dePaola's real Italian grandmother; she is Nana Fall-River in *The Baby Sister* and Grandmother in *Watch Out for the Chicken Feet in Your Soup.*

5. Bette Peltola's remarks appear in *Tomie dePaola: A Portfolio,* prepared by the 1990 United States Board on Books for Young People's Andersen Committee and G. P. Putnam's Sons for presentation to the International Board on Books for Young People's Hans Christian Andersen International Jury.

6. Leonardo da Vinci (1452-1519), *Mona Lisa,* Musée du Louvre, Paris.

## STORY MAKING

1. Henri Rousseau (1844-1910), *The Sleeping Gypsy,* Museum of Modern Art, New York City.

2. Pablo Picasso (1881-1973), *The Old Guitarist,* The Art Institute, Chicago.

3. An Ernest Hemingway-type character is the protagonist in John Cech's *The Southernmost Cat,* (Simon & Schuster). Claude Monet is referred to as "the old painter in the straw hat" in Joan Sweeney's *Once Upon a Lily Pad,* (Chronicle Books).

4. Henri Matisse and Pablo Picasso were friends, but history also attests to their frequent quarrels about art—noted in Patrick O'Brian's *Picasso: A Biography,* (Putnam).

5. Claude Monet, Josephine Baker, Isadora Duncan, Zelda Fitzgerald, and Ernest Hemingway are a few of the characters appearing in Gertrude's (Stein) and Alice's (B. Toklas) salon.

6. Georges Braque (1882-1963), *Still Life with Score by Satie,* Georges Pompidou Centre, Paris.

7. DePaola's one-time cat Satie was named after the composer Erik Satie. DePaola had driven to the airport in Manchester to pick up his cat, which was being shipped from New York. Music by Satie was playing on dePaola's car radio, motivating him to call the cat Satie.

8. McGovern's *Nicholas Bentley Stoningpot III* was originally entitled first *Nicky's Island,* and then *Nicky Lost and Found,* according to material at the Kerlan Collection, an internationally recognized center of research in the field of children's literature, University of Minnesota, Minneapolis.

9. Tamas Hofer and Edit Fel, *Hungarian Folk Art.* New York: Oxford University Press, 1979.

## INFORMATIONAL BOOKS

1. The quote couldn't be located, and dePaola no longer remembers its source. As a first-time illustrator, however, he keenly felt the words; now, in retrospect, he finds them "highly complimentary."

2. The Kerlan Collection holds most of dePaola's early manuscripts and artwork up to the mid-1970s as well as some later work.

3. Jon Scieszka and Lane Smith's *The Stinky Cheese Man* (Viking) uses just the words "title page" in very large type on the title page, has the dedication upside down, and hypes itself on the front flap copy; Fred Marcellino's *Puss in Boots* (Farrar, Straus) has the title on the back jacket as does Maurice Sendak's *We Are All in the Dumps with Jack and Guy* (HarperCollins).

4. The Children's Book Showcase, sponsored by The Children's Book Council from 1972 to 1977, was an informational project to celebrate creative approaches to design and production in the children's book field. Catalogs were published annually.

5. Other Holiday House books in this quintet were *The Kids' Cat Book, The Family Christmas Tree Book, The Quicksand Book,* and *The Popcorn Book.*

6. Information from Holiday House publicity files.

## MOTHER GOOSE AND OTHER COLLECTIONS

1. Robert D. Hale, "Musings," *The Horn Book Magazine,* November/December 1985.

2. Emily Dickinson lived from 1830-1886. Because she was reclusive, almost all of her poems were published after her death.

3. The Illustrators' Exhibition is held annually at the Children's Book Fair, Bologna, Italy.

4. Joy Backhouse, the children's editor at Methuen Children's Books Ltd., was dePaola's London editor; *Tomie dePaola's Mother Goose* was published in England in 1985.

5. Nanette Stevenson was art director at Putnam from July 1981 to February 1994.

6. Iona and Peter Opie, *The Oxford Nursery Rhyme Book.* London: Oxford University Press, 1955, preface.

7. Julie Cummins, ed. *Children's Book Illustration and Design,* New York: Library of Applied Design, 1972.

8. The early version dePaola remembers is probably *The Real Mother Goose,* illustrated by Blanche Fisher Wright. New York: Macmillan/Checkerboard, 1916.

9. Statistics were supplied by Putnam's royalty department in December 1997.

10. Hale, *The Horn Book Magazine.*

11. *Tomie's Little Mother Goose,* a board book, became an immediate bestseller in 1997.

12. Hale, *The Horn Book Magazine.*

13. Patrick Collins was a designer at Putnam from January 1990 to January 1997; Arthur Levine was an editor at Putnam from 1984 to 1987 and from 1990 to 1994; Nora Cohen served as editor in various capacities at Putnam from 1977 to 1990.

## PATTERNS, VISUAL THEMES, AND MOTIFS

1. Alice Perry, "Joys of Christmas Dance in His Head," *Concord Monitor,* November 26, 1980.

2. Corita Kent, also known as Sister Corita, was part of a contemporary liturgical art movement in the late 1950s and early 1960s; after she left the convent, she signed her work "Corita."

3. Sketches and accompanying notes for *Helga's Dowry* and for *Big Anthony and the Magic Ring* are at the Kerlan Collection, University of Minnesota, Minneapolis.

4. Jean François Millet (1814-1875), The Angelus, Musée d'Orsay, Paris.

5. Tomie dePaola, "From an Artist/Author," *Language Arts,* April, 1981.

6. Pieter Brueghel the Elder (1525/30-1569), *Children's Games,* Kunsthistorisches Museum, Vienna; Joachim de Patinir (1485-1524), *Landscape with St. Jerome Removing the Thorn from the Lion's Paw,* Museo del Prado, Madrid; The Bayeux Tapestry, Centre Guillaume le Conquérant, Bayeux, France, are examples of sequencing in medieval masterworks.

## PUBLISHING HISTORY

1. Blanche Gregory, of Blanche C. Gregory Inc., represented adult authors such as Joyce Carol Oates.

2. The Agents' Guild was an organization for people who represented authors and artists in publishing.

3. Bernice Kohn Hunt, freelance editor of the Science Is What and Why series, is also the author of many children's books including *The Whatchamacallit Book*, illustrated by Tomie dePaola, (Putnam).

4. Freedman, *Holiday House: The First Fifty Years.*

5. Mary Gordon is the author of *Final Payments* (Viking) and other books for adults.

6. *The Quicksand Book* quote was from an unnamed reviewer in the Los Angeles school system.

7. David Macaulay is the author of *Cathedral, City, Pyramid,* and the Caldecott Medal book *Black and White,* published by Houghton Mifflin.

8. In the preseparation process the artist separates the color by preparing a keyplate and one or more overlays; each color requires a separate overlay; when printed, they form a multicolor picture.

9. Peter Israel was CEO of Putnam from 1978 to 1987.

10. Johnnie L. Roberts, "King of the Deal," *Newsweek,* June 12, 1995.

11. Whitebird Books:

   *The Little Snowgirl, An Old Russian Tale,* adapted and illustrated by Carolyn Croll, 1989

   *Tony's Bread, An Italian Folktale,* written and illustrated by Tomie dePaola, 1989

   *The Badger and the Magic Fan, A Japanese Folktale,* adapted by Tony Johnston, illustrated by Tomie dePaola, 1990

   *Good Morning, Granny Rose, An Arkansas Folktale,* retold and illustrated by Warren Ludwig, 1990

   *Quail Song, A Pueblo Indian Tale,* adapted by Valerie Scho Carey, illustrated by Ivan Barnett, 1990

   *The Stonecutter, An Indian Folktale,* retold and illustrated by Pam Newton, 1990

   *Old Noah's Elephants, An Israeli Folktale,* adapted and illustrated by Warren Ludwig, 1991

   *The Three Brothers, A German Folktale,* adapted and illustrated by Carolyn Croll, 1991

   *Chancay and the Secret of Fire, A Peruvian Folktale,* written and illustrated by Donald Charles, 1992

   *The Green Gourd, A North Carolina Folktale,* retold by C. W. Hunter, illustrated by Tony Griego, 1992

   *Jamie O'Rourke and the Big Potato, An Irish Folktale,* retold and illustrated by Tomie dePaola, 1992

   *The Singing Fir Tree, A Swiss Folktale,* retold by Marti Stone, illustrated by Barry Root, 1992

   *The Legend of the Persian Carpet,* retold by Tomie dePaola, illustrated by Claire Ewart, 1993

   *Magic Spring, A Korean Folktale,* retold and illustrated by Nami Rhee, 1993

   *The Rooster Who Went to His Uncle's Wedding, A Latin American Folktale,* retold by Alma Flor Ada, illustrated by Kathleen Kuchera, 1993

   *Under the Midsummer Sky, A Swedish Folktale,* written by Cole Lexa Schafer, illustrated by Pat Geddes, 1994

12. Frith and dePaola's remarks about the beginnings of Whitebird Books are adapted from an interview in the May 1, 1980 issue of *Booklist*; information about its folding came from an interview in 1997.

## CREATING THE BOOK

1. Silvey, Anita, ed. *Children's Books and Their Creators.* Boston: Houghton Mifflin, 1995.

2. Cecilia Yung is currently art director at Putnam; Donna Mark was a senior designer 1991-1999.

3. Sketches, drawings, and manuscript are from early drafts of *Big Anthony, His Story,* published by Putnam in 1998.

## DEPAOLA OFF PAGE

1.  DePaola was contacted by the marketing department at Neiman-Marcus and asked to design their 1982 Christmas shopping bag and catalog cover.

2.  Raymond Teague, "Writer-Artist Brings Bluebonnet Legend to Children of Texas," *Fort Worth Star Telegram,* April 7, 1983.

3.  DePaola designed the Dayton's-Bachman's Annual Flower Show in 1989.

4.  The Popcorn Factory, 13970 West Laurel Dr., Lake Forest, Illinois 60045, offers a combination of caramel, cheddar cheese, and butter or just butter popcorn in tin gallon containers; dePaola has created various designs for the company over the years.

5.  The dePaola giftware collection from Midwest of Cannon Falls, 32057 64th Avenue, PO Box 20, Cannon Falls, Minnesota 55009, debuted in 1995.

6.  DePaola created a Strega Nona cover to celebrate the fifth anniversary (July, 1996) of *Book Links: Connecting Books, Libraries, and Classrooms,* edited by Barbara Elleman and published by the American Library Association, covers for the Lands' End Catalogs, Holiday 1992 and the Early Spring 1997 issues, and covers for *Cricket* and *Baby Bug,* published by the Carus group. The photo essay appeared in *Country Home,* December, 1992.

7.  The Children's Theatre Company, 2400 Third Avenue South, Minneapolis, Minnesota 55404, presented *The Clown of God,* directed by John Clark Donahue, which ran from February 28 through April 5, 1981, to sold-out houses.

8.  Peter Vaughan, "Not Just Child's Play," *Minneapolis Star,* February 27, 1981.

9.  Vaughan, *Minneapolis Star.*

10. Mike Steele, "Children's Theatre Offers *Clown of God" Minneapolis Tribune,* March 2, 1981.

11. New Hampshire Philharmonic Orchestra, which occasionally performs at the Capitol Center for the Arts in Concord, New Hampshire, is directed by Patrick Botti, who became aware of dePaola's books through reading them to his young children. "With dePaola providing words and pictures, Botti says that his imagination can't help but supply the music." Christine Hamm, "A Musical Twist to Story Time," *Concord Monitor,* May 29, 1997.

12. DePaola has appeared on *Barney and Friends* (PBS) Episodes 209, featuring *The Art Lesson;* 314, featuring *"Charlie Needs a Cloak";* and 418, featuring *The Baby Sister.*

13. Dana Wormald, "Story Time with Tomie dePaola," *Concord Monitor,* December 11, 1997.

14. Mary Ann Esposito, *Celebrations, Italian Style.* New York: Hearst, 1995; the author is the host of *Ciao Italia* (PBS).

15. Food Research and Action Center (FRAC) held its twenty-fifth anniversary dinner in Washington, D.C., on June 7, 1995.

16. Guy Kawasaki, *How to Drive Your Competition Crazy.* New York: Hyperion, 1995.

17. *The Knight and the Dragon* was reformatted and reproduced in *Crayola Kids,* March 1997.

18. Read Across America, sponsored by The National Education Association, was celebrated on March 2, 1998, with dePaola participating in programs with New Hampshire's governor and speaking on National Public Radio's *All Things Considered.* He also created a logo design for a Certificate of Participation for the celebrations in 1998 and 1999.

19. DePaola's Children's Book Week poster, "1983—Get Into Books," can be found in *75 Years of Children's Book Week Posters,* with an introduction by Leonard Marcus. New York: Knopf, 1994.

20. Soft dolls of She-Who-Is-Alone, Strega Nona, and Maggie's Monster are produced by MerryMakers Inc., Suite 201, 6239 College Avenue, Oakland, California 94618.

21. Rubber stamps of angels, cats, and other dePaola figures are manufactured by Kidstamps, PO Box 18699, Cleveland Heights, Ohio 44118.

22. The Advent calendars featuring dePaola's art were printed by WJ Fantasy Inc., 955 Connecticut Avenue, Bridgeport, Connecticut 06607; the floor puzzle containing an image from *Tomie dePaola's Book of Bible Stories* was issued by Harper's Fare.

23. DePaola books on CD-ROM include *The Art Lesson* and *Big Anthony's Mixed-up Magic,* based on *Strega Nona Meets Her Match.*

24. Sherry Litwack, Hollyhock Press. 1575 Monument Street, Concord, Massachusetts 01742.

25. Val Z. Hornburg. *On the Wing of a Whitebird: A Tomie dePaola Resource Book,* PO Box 3483, Portland, Oregon 97208.

26. Ronne Hartfield, director of education for The Art Institute of Chicago, arranged for an exhibition of dePaola's artwork to inaugurate the Thoresen Galley in The Kraft Education Center in the Art Institute of Chicago. It ran from September 1992 through January 1993.

27. Lesley Wright, exhibition coordinator, Cedar Rapids Museum of Art, 410 Third Avenue SE, Cedar Rapids, Iowa 52401.

28. Interview with Jane Kerr, public relations director, Rock County Historical Society Museum, 10 S. High Street, Janesville, Wisconsin 53547.

29. Jan Bruton and Lynn Kelly were owners of A Children's Place, a bookstore in Portland, Oregon; Jim Roginski, "Portland Bookseller Organizes a Parade in Honor of Tomie dePaola's Visit," *Publishers Weekly,* July 23, 1982.

30. DePaola spent eleven days in the Modesto, California, schools as author-in-residence as part of their Arts Appreciation Program, meeting with almost 8,500 children in 23 schools.

31. Children's Book Council of Australia, Fourth National Conference, "Time Will Tell: Children's Literature into the 21st Century," May 22-24, 1998.

32. *Down Under & Over Here*, an original art show, opened at the Cedar Rapids Museum of Art in March 1998.

33. Ellie Ferriter, "This Is Dedicated To..." *New Hampshire Sunday News,* February 9, 1997.

34. Ellie Ferriter, "Christmas with dePaola," *New Hampshire Sunday News,* December 24-25, 1994.

35. DePaola donates copies of each of his books to The Tomie dePaola Room in New London's Tracy Memorial Library.

36. DePaola became acquainted with the librarians at Richards Free Library in Newport, New Hampshire, the home of Sarah Josepha Hale, while researching the art for *Mary Had a Little Lamb*; the book is dedicated to Jean Michie Galloway and Anne Purnell, then librarians in Newport. An original painting from the book hangs in the library.

37. "Tomie dePaola Celebration" booklet. September 13-15, 1985, Meriden, Connecticut.

38. Allen Raymond, "Two Towns Throw a Party," *Teaching K-8,* August/September 1993.

39. The video *A Visit with Tomie dePaola*, was produced in 1996; *Tomie dePaola, Live in Concert* was produced in 1999. They are available through Whitebird, Inc., 300 County Road, New London, New Hampshire 03257.

## DEPAOLA'S NON-BOOK ART

1. Deborah McKew, "Talking with Tomie dePaola," Upper Valley Magazine, November/December 1992.

2. DePaola's fine-art serigraphs, rag paper on canvas, are numbered and hand signed, and produced by Beacon Fine Arts, 49 Morton Place, Jersey City, New Jersey 07305. For the galleries handling these prints, consult http://www.bingley.com, or call 1-800-700-1205.

3. *Tomie dePaola's Other Side* was an exhibit at Colby-Sawyer College in 1991.

4. Roger Crossgrove is a lifelong friend. One of dePaola's early painting teachers, he taught at Pratt Institute for fifteen years, before becoming head of the art department at the University of Connecticut, where he is now Professor Emeritus.

# Major Awards, Events, and Recognitions

1958. Exhibits at first group show (non-book art), South Vermont Art Center, Manchester, Vermont

1961. Exhibits at first one-man show (non-book art), The Botolph Group, Boston

1965. Illustrates first book, *Sound,* by Lisa Miller, Coward-McCann

1966. Writes and illustrates *The Wonderful Dragon of Timlin,* Bobbs-Merrill

1968. Receives Award of Excellence, Art Directors' Club of Boston

1969. Receives Silver Award, Franklin Prize Competition, Franklin Typographers, New York

1970. Exhibits *Journey of the Kiss* artwork in the American Institute of Graphic Arts of Outstanding Children's Books

1972. Publishes first full-color book, *The Wind and the Sun,* Ginn

1974. Receives first Notable Children's Book citation for *"Charlie Needs a Cloak"* from the American Library Association/Association for Library Service to Children

1976. Receives Caldecott Honor Book award for *Strega Nona*

1977. Receives second place, Japan's Owl Prize, for *Strega Nona*

1977. Exhibits at *Twelfth Exhibition of Original Pictures of International Children's Picture Books,* sponsored by Maruzen Co., Ltd., and Shiko-Sha Co., Ltd., Japan

1978. Exhibits at Illustrators' Exhibition, Children's Book Fair, Bologna, Italy

1978. Receives The Nakamori Prize, Japan, for *Strega Nona*

1978. Receives the American Institute of Graphic Arts Award for *Helga's Dowry*

1978. Exhibits *The Clown of God* and *Pancakes for Breakfast* at the Twenty-ninth International Exhibition of Children's and Youth Books, International Youth Library, Munich, Germany

1979. *Bill and Pete, The Clown of God, Four Scary Stories, Jamie's Tiger, Pancakes for Breakfast,* and *The Popcorn Book* are selected for Children's Choices, International Reading Association/ The Children's Book Council

1980. Exhibits at the first *The Original Art* exhibition, Master Eagle Gallery, New York City

1980. Wins the Garden State Children's Book Award for younger nonfiction from the New Jersey Library Association for *The Quicksand Book*

1980. Appointed to Board of Directors, Society of Children's Book Writers and Illustrators, on which he still serves

1981. Opens *The Clown of God* at the Children's Theatre Company in Minneapolis

1981. Receives Kerlan Award for "singular attainment in children's literature," University of Minnesota, Minneapolis

1982. Exhibits at *A Decade of the Original Art of the Best Illustrated Children's Books, 1970-1980,* University of Connecticut Library, Storrs, Connecticut

1982. Receives a Boston Globe-Horn Book Honor award for *The Friendly Beasts*

1982. Designs Christmas catalog cover and shopping bag for Neiman-Marcus department stores

1982. Receives Golden Kite Award for Illustration, Society of Children's Book Writers and Illustrators, for *Giorgio's Village*

1983. Receives Critici in Erba commendation from the Bologna Biennale for *The Friendly Beasts* at the Children's Book Fair, Bologna, Italy

1983. Receives Regina Medal, Catholic Library Association, "in recognition of outstanding accomplishments in the field of children's literature"

1983. Exhibits at Twenty-fifth Annual Exhibition, Society of Illustrators, New York City

1983. Designs Children's Book Week poster, "Get Into Books" for The Children's Book Council

1983. Designs first of several popcorn cans for The Popcorn Factory

1985. Exhibits artwork for *Tattie's River Journey,* by Shirley Rousseau Murphy, at the Biennale of Illustration, Bratislava

1985. Receives Doctor of Letters, Honoris Causa, Colby-Sawyer College, New London, New Hampshire

1986. Signs global agreement with Putnam

1986. Receives David McCord Children's Literature Citation, first recipient, for "significant contribution to excellence in books for children," sponsored by Framingham State College and the Nobscot Reading Council of the International Reading Association, Framingham, Massachusetts

1987. Exhibits books and non-book art, *Tomie dePaola: A Retrospective* at Arts and Science Center, Nashua, New Hampshire

1987. Receives Golden Kite Honor for Illustration, Society of Children's Book Writers and Illustrators, for Carolyn Craven's *What the Mailman Brought*

1990. Named U.S. nominee for the Hans Christian Andersen Award in Illustration given by the International Board on Books for Young People

1990. Receives Smithson Medal, Smithsonian Institution

1990. Opens *Tomie dePaola's Mother Goose* at The Children's Theatre Company in Minneapolis

1991. Dedicates The Tomie dePaola Room, Tracy Memorial Library, New London, New Hampshire

1992. Opens the new Thoresen Gallery in The Kraft Education Center in The Art Institute of Chicago, with a one-man show

1993. Receives Helen Keating Ott Award, Church and Synagogue Library Association

1993. Creates an annual art scholarship in his hometown of Meriden, Connecticut

1993. Appears on *Barney and Friends*, the first children's illustrator to be on the program

1994. Receives Doctor of Humane Letters, Honoris Causa, Saint Anselm College, Manchester, New Hampshire

1995. Exhibits *Tomie Turns 60* at Cedar Rapids Museum of Art, Cedar Rapids, Iowa

1995. Receives University of Southern Mississippi Medallion for total body of work, Hattiesburg, Mississippi

1995. Issues Midwest of Cannon Falls's Tomie dePaola Giftware line

1995. Opens a non-book art show at Cove Gallery, Wellfleet, Massachusetts, and *Tomie's Other Side* at Sawyer Center, Colby-Sawyer College, New London, New Hampshire

1995. Presents autographed copy of signed, numbered, limited-edition poster created for Food Research and Action Center to First Lady Hillary Clinton

1996. Receives Doctor of Humane Letters, Honoris Causa, Notre Dame College, Manchester, New Hampshire

1996. Receives Milner Award, Atlanta Fulton Public Library, Atlanta, Georgia

1997. Is a guest at the White House for an event honoring the Reading Is Fundamental National Poster Contest winner and the National RIF Reader

1997. Named a Literary Light, Associates of the Boston Public Library, Boston, Massachusetts

1998. Receives the Keene State College Children's Literature Festival Award, Keene, New Hampshire

1998. Begins publishing serigraphs with Beacon Fine Arts

1998. Presents keynote speech, Children's Book Council of Australia, Fourth National Conference

1999. Publishes first chapter book, *26 Fairmount Avenue* (Putnam)

1999. Bestows the Northeast Children's Literature Collection at the Thomas J. Dodd Research Center at the University of Connecticut with his backlist manuscripts and art, which is celebrated with a two-day festival

1999. *Strega Nona* and *The Art Lesson* are among the 100 books selected for Read Across America, a National Education Association initiative to promote reading among children

1999. Receives Doctor of Fine Arts, Honoris Causa, University of Connecticut, Storrs, Connecticut

1999. Selected as one of "100 People Who Shaped the Century" in New Hampshire by *Concord Monitor*

# Bibliography

TITLES WRITTEN (OR EDITED) AND ILLUSTRATED
BY TOMIE DEPAOLA

Andy, That's My Name. Prentice-Hall, 1973

The Art Lesson. Putnam, 1989

The Baby Sister. Putnam, 1996

Baby's First Christmas. Putnam, 1988

Big Anthony and the Magic Ring. Harcourt Brace Jovanovich, 1979

Big Anthony, His Story. Putnam, 1998

Bill and Pete. Putnam, 1978

Bill and Pete Go Down the Nile. Putnam, 1987

Bill and Pete to the Rescue. Putnam, 1998

Bonjour, Mr. Satie. Putnam, 1991

The Bubble Factory. Grosset & Dunlap, 1996

The Cat on the Dovrefell. Putnam, 1979

"Charlie Needs a Cloak." Prentice-Hall, 1973

The Christmas Pageant. Winston Press, 1978

Christopher, the Holy Giant. Holiday House, 1994

The Cloud Book. Holiday House, 1975

The Clown of God. Harcourt Brace Jovanovich, 1978

The Comic Adventures of Old Mother Hubbard and Her Dog. Harcourt Brace Jovanovich, 1981

Country Angel Christmas. Putnam, 1995

David and Goliath. Winston, 1984

Days of the Blackbird. Putnam, 1997

An Early American Christmas. Holiday House, 1987

The Family Christmas Tree Book. Holiday House, 1980

Fight the Night. Lippincott, 1968

Fin M'Coul, the Giant of Knockmany Hill. Holiday House, 1981

The First Christmas: A Pop-Up Book. Putnam, 1984

Flicks. Harcourt Brace Jovanovich, 1979

Four Stories for Four Seasons. Prentice-Hall, 1977

Francis, the Poor Man of Assisi. Holiday House, 1982

The Friendly Beasts. Putnam, 1981

Get Dressed, Santa! Grosset & Dunlap, 1996

Giorgio's Village: A Pop-up Book. Putnam, 1982

Haircuts for the Woolseys. Putnam, 1989

Helga's Dowry: A Troll Love Story. Harcourt Brace Jovanovich, 1977

The Hunter and the Animals. Holiday House, 1981

Jamie O'Rourke and the Big Potato. Putnam/Whitebird, 1992

Jingle, the Christmas Clown. Putnam, 1992

Joe and the Snow. Hawthorn, 1968

The Journey of the Kiss. Hawthorn, 1970

The Kids' Cat Book. Holiday House, 1979

Kit and Kat. Grosset & Dunlap, 1994

The Knight and the Dragon. Putnam, 1980

The Lady of Guadalupe. Holiday House, 1980

The Legend of Old Befana. Harcourt Brace Jovanovich, 1980

The Legend of the Bluebonnet. Putnam, 1983

The Legend of the Indian Paintbrush. Putnam, 1988

The Legend of the Poinsettia. Putnam, 1994

Little Grunt and the Big Egg. Holiday House, 1990

Marianna May and Nursey. Holiday House, 1983

Mary, the Mother of Jesus. Holiday House, 1995

Merry Christmas, Strega Nona. Harcourt Brace Jovanovich, 1986

Michael Bird-Boy. Prentice-Hall, 1975

The Miracles of Jesus. Holiday House, 1987

The Monsters' Ball. Hawthorn, 1970

My First Chanukah. Putnam, 1989

My First Easter. Putnam, 1990

My First Halloween. Putnam, 1991

My First Passover. Putnam, 1990

My First Thanksgiving. Putnam, 1992

The Mysterious Giant of Barletta. Harcourt Brace Jovanovich, 1984

Nana Upstairs & Nana Downstairs. Putnam, 1973

Nana Upstairs & Nana Downstairs, new edition. Putnam, 1998

The Night of Las Posadas. Putnam, 1999

Noah and the Ark. Winston, 1983

Now One Foot, Now the Other. Putnam, 1981

Oliver Button Is a Sissy. Harcourt Brace Jovanovich, 1979

Pancakes for Breakfast. Harcourt Brace Jovanovich, 1978

The Parables of Jesus. Holiday House, 1987

Parker Pig, Esquire. Hawthorn, 1969

Patrick, Patron Saint of Ireland. Holiday House, 1992

The Popcorn Book. Holiday House, 1978

The Prince of the Dolomites. Harcourt Brace Jovanovich, 1980

Queen Esther. Harper & Row, 1986

The Quicksand Book. Holiday House, 1977

Sing, Pierrot, Sing. Harcourt Brace Jovanovich, 1983

Songs of the Fog Maiden. Holiday House, 1979

The Story of the Three Wise Kings. Putnam, 1983

Strega Nona. Prentice-Hall, 1975

Strega Nona, Her Story. Putnam, 1996

Strega Nona Meets Her Match. Putnam, 1993

Strega Nona's Magic Lessons. Harcourt Brace Jovanovich, 1982

Things to Make and Do for Valentine's Day. Franklin Watts, 1976

Tom. Putnam, 1993

Tomie dePaola's Book of Bible Stories. Putnam/Zondervan, 1990

Tomie dePaola's Book of Christmas Carols. Putnam, 1987

Tomie dePaola's Book of Poems. Putnam, 1988

Tomie dePaola's Book of the Old Testament (Old Testament text with illustrations from Tomie dePaola's Book of Bible Stories). Putnam, 1995

Tomie dePaola's Country Farm. Putnam, 1984

Tomie dePaola's Favorite Nursery Tales. Putnam, 1986

Tomie dePaola's Kitten Kids. (Katie, Kit and Cousin Tom; Pajamas for Kit; Katie and Kit at the Beach; Katie's Good Idea). Simon & Schuster, 1986

Tomie dePaola's Make Your Own Christmas Cards Book. Price Stern Sloan, 1998

Tomie dePaola's Mother Goose. Putnam, 1985

Tomie dePaola's Mother Goose Story Streamers. Putnam, 1984

Tomie's Little Mother Goose. Putnam, 1997

Tony's Bread. Putnam/Whitebird, 1989

Too Many Hopkins. Putnam, 1989

26 Fairmount Avenue. Putnam, 1999

The Unicorn and the Moon. Ginn, 1973

Watch Out for the Chicken Feet in Your Soup. Prentice-Hall, 1974

When Everyone Was Fast Asleep. Holiday House, 1976

The Wind and the Sun. Ginn, 1972

The Wonderful Dragon of Timlin. Bobbs-Merrill, 1966


## TITLES ILLUSTRATED BY TOMIE DEPAOLA (UNLESS OTHERWISE NOTED)

Adler, David A. The Carsick Zebra and Other Animal Riddles. Holiday House, 1983

Alexander, Sue. Marc the Magnificent. Pantheon, 1978

Alexenberg, Melvin L. Light and Sight. Prentice-Hall, 1969

——. Sound Science. Prentice-Hall, 1968

Andersen, Hans Christian. The Emperor's New Clothes: An All-Star Retelling of the Classic Fairy Tale, illustrated by Tomie dePaola et al. Harcourt Brace, 1998

Baker, Sanna Anderson. Who's a Friend of the Water-Spurting Whale. David C. Cook, 1987

Balestrino, Philip. Hot As an Ice Cube. Crowell, 1971

Belpré, Pura, reteller. The Tiger and the Rabbit, and Other Tales. Lippincott, 1965

Bennett, Jill. Teeny Tiny. Putnam, 1986

The Big Book for Our Planet, illustrated by Tomie dePaola et al. Dutton, 1993

Bly, Robert. The Morning Glory. Kayak Books, 1969

Boylan, Eleanor. How to Be a Puppeteer. McCall Publishing, 1970

Calhoun, Mary. Old Man Whickutt's Donkey. Parents' Magazine Press, 1975

Coerr, Eleanor. The Mixed-up Mystery Smell. Putnam, 1976

Cohen, Peter Zachary. Authorized Autumn Charts of the Upper Red Canoe River Country. Atheneum, 1972

Cole, William, selector. Oh, Such Foolishness! Lippincott, 1978

Craven, Carolyn. What the Mailman Brought. Putnam, 1987

Davies, Valentine. Miracle on 34th Street. Harcourt Brace Jovanovich, 1984

Eichner, James A. The Cabinet of the President of the United States. Franklin Watts, 1968

Emrich, Duncan, selector. The Folklore of Love and Courtship. American Heritage Press, 1970

——. The Folklore of Weddings and Marriage. American Heritage Press, 1970

Epstein, Sam and Beryl. Hold Everything. Holiday House, 1973

——. Look in the Mirror. Holiday House, 1973

——. Pick It Up. Holiday House, 1971

——. Take This Hammer. Hawthorn, 1969

——. Who Needs Holes? Hawthorn, 1970

Ernst, Kathryn F. Danny and His Thumb. Prentice-Hall, 1973

Farber, Norma. Six Impossible Things before Breakfast, illustrated by Tomie dePaola et al. Addison-Wesley, 1977

———. This Is the Ambulance Leaving the Zoo. Dutton, 1975

Fisher, John. John Fisher's Magic Book. Prentice-Hall, 1971

For Our Children, illustrated by Tomie dePaola et al. Disney Press, 1991

Fritz, Jean. Can't You Make Them Behave, King George? Coward-McCann, 1977

———. Shh! We're Writing the Constitution. Putnam, 1987

———. The Good Giants and the Bad Pukwudgies. Putnam, 1982

———. The Great Adventure of Christopher Columbus: A Pop-up Book. Putnam/Grosset, 1992

Gauch, Patricia Lee. The Little Friar Who Flew. Putnam, 1980

———. Once Upon a Dinkelsbühl. Putnam, 1977

The GOSH ABC Book, illustrated by Tomie dePaola et al. Aurum, 1988

Graham, John. I Love You, Mouse. Harcourt Brace Jovanovich, 1976

Hale, Sarah Josepha. Mary Had a Little Lamb. Holiday House, 1984

Hall, Malcolm. Edward, Benjamin & Butter. Coward-McCann, 1981

Hancock, Sibyl. Mario's Mystery Machine. Putnam, 1972

Hardendorff, Jeanne B. Tricky Peik and Other Picture Tales. Lippincott, 1967

Hopkins, Lee Bennett, selector. Beat the Drum, Independence Day Has Come. Harcourt Brace Jovanovich, 1977

———. Easter Buds Are Springing. Harcourt Brace Jovanovich, 1979

———. Good Morning to You, Valentine. Harcourt Brace Jovanovich, 1976

Houselander, Caryll. Petook: An Easter Story. Holiday House, 1988

Hunt, Bernice Kohn. The Whatchamacallit Book. Putnam, 1976

Jacobs, Leland Blair. Poetry for Chuckles and Grins. Garrard, 1968

Jane, Mary C. The Rocking-Chair Ghost. Lippincott, 1969

Jennings, Michael. Robin Goodfellow and the Giant Dwarf. McGraw-Hill, 1981

Johnston, Tony. Alice Nizzy Nazzy: The Witch of Sante Fe. Putnam, 1995

———. The Badger and the Magic Fan. Putnam/Whitebird, 1990

———. Four Scary Stories. Putnam, 1978

———. Odd Jobs. Putnam, 1977

———. Odd Jobs and Friends. Putnam, 1982

———. Pages of Music. Putnam, 1988

———. The Quilt Story. Putnam, 1985

———. The Tale of Rabbit and Coyote. Putnam, 1994

———. The Vanishing Pumpkin. Putnam, 1983

Keller, Charles, and Richard Baker. The Star-Spangled Banana and Other Revolutionary Riddles. Prentice-Hall, 1974

Kroll, Steven. Fat Magic. Holiday House, 1978

———. Santa's Crash-Bang Christmas. Holiday House, 1977

———. The Tyrannosaurus Game. Holiday House, 1976

Lewis, Naomi, reteller. The Flying Trunk and Other Stories from Andersen, illustrated by Tomie dePaola et al. Andersen Press, 1986

Lexau, Joan M. Finders Keepers, Losers Weepers. Lippincott, 1967

Low, Alice. David's Windows. Putnam, 1974

McGovern, Ann. Nicholas Bentley Stoningpot III. Holiday House, 1982

MacLachlan, Patricia. Moon, Stars, Frogs and Friends. Pantheon, 1980

Madrigal, Antonio Hernández, reteller. The Eagle and the Rainbow. Fulcrum, 1997

———. Erandi's Braids. Putnam, 1999

Miller, Lisa. Sound. Coward-McCann, 1965

———. Wheels. Coward-McCann, 1965

Moore, Clement C. The Night Before Christmas. Holiday House, 1980

Mooser, Stephen. Funnyman and the Penny Dodo. Franklin Watts, 1984

———. Funnyman's First Case. Franklin Watts, 1981

———. The Ghost with the Halloween Hiccups. Franklin Watts, 1977

Murphy, Shirley Rousseau. Tattie's River Journey. Dial, 1983

O'Connor, Jane. Benny's Big Bubble. Grosset & Dunlap, 1997

Once Upon a Time: A RIF Book, written and illustrated by Tomie dePaola et al. Putnam, 1986

Pandell, Karen. I Love You, Sun; I Love You, Moon. Putnam, 1994

Pinkwater, Daniel M. The Wuggie Norple Story. Four Winds Press, 1980

Pitt, Valerie. Let's Find Out about Communications. Franklin Watts, 1973

Prager, Annabelle. The Spooky Halloween Party. Pantheon, 1981

———. The Surprise Party. Pantheon, 1977

Rinkoff, Barbara. Rutherford T Finds 21B. Putnam, 1970

Rose, Anne. The Triumphs of Fuzzy Fogtop. Dial, 1979

Rosenbaum, Jean, and Lutie McAuliffe. What Is Fear? Prentice-Hall, 1972

Salus, Naomi Panush. My Daddy's Mustache. Doubleday, 1979

Saunders, Rubie. The Franklin Watts Concise Guide to Baby-Sitting. Franklin Watts, 1972

Schneider, Nina. Hercules, the Gentle Giant. Hawthorn, 1969

Shapiro, Arnold L. Mice Squeak, We Speak. Putnam, 1997

Shapp, Martha and Charles. Let's Find Out About Houses. Franklin Watts, 1975

———. Let's Find Out About Summer. Franklin Watts, 1976

To Ride a Butterfly, written and illustrated by Tomie dePaola et al. Bantam Doubleday Dell, 1991

Wahl, Jan. Jamie's Tiger. Harcourt Brace Jovanovich, 1978

Wallace, Daisy, selector. Ghost Poems. Holiday House, 1979

Ward, Cindy. Cookie's Week. Putnam, 1988

Watson, Pauline. The Walking Coat. Walker, 1980

Weiss, Malcolm E. Solomon Grundy, Born on Oneday: A Finite Arithmetic Puzzle. Crowell, 1977

Willard, Nancy. The Mountains of Quilt. Harcourt Brace Jovanovich, 1987

———. Simple Pictures Are Best. Harcourt Brace Jovanovich, 1977

Williams, Barbara. If He's My Brother. Harvey House, 1976

Winthrop, Elizabeth. Maggie and the Monster. Holiday House, 1987

Wise, William. Monsters of the Middle Ages. Putnam, 1971

Yeomans, Thomas. For Every Child a Star. Holiday House, 1986

Yolen, Jane. The Giants' Farm. Seabury Press, 1977

———. The Giants Go Camping. Seabury Press, 1979

———. Hark! A Christmas Sampler. Putnam, 1991


## BOOKS WRITTEN BY DEPAOLA, ILLUSTRATED BY OTHERS

Criss-Cross Applesauce, illustrated by B. A. King and his children. Addison House, 1978

The Legend of the Persian Carpet, illustrated by Claire Ewart. Whitebird/Putnam, 1993


NOTE: DePaola's books have been translated into more than 15 languages.

# Art Notes

The medium for the illustrations reproduced in this book is given after each title.

26 Fairmount Avenue–Black line and wash

Alice Nizzy Nazzy–Acrylics

Andy, That's My Name–Three-color preseparated art

The Art Lesson–Rotring Artist Colors

The Baby Sister–Rotring Artist Colors

Big Anthony and the Magic Ring–Rotring Artist Colors and pencil

Big Anthony, His Story–Rotring Artist Colors

Bill and Pete–Four-color preseparated art

Bill and Pete to the Rescue–Transparent acrylics

Bonjour, Mr. Satie–Acrylics

"Charlie Needs a Cloak"–Three-color preseparated art

Christopher, the Holy Giant–Acrylics

The Cloud Book–Three-color preseparated art

The Clown of God–Watercolors, colored inks, and pencil

Country Angel Christmas–Acrylics

Days of the Blackbird–Acrylics

An Early American Christmas–Rotring Artist Colors and pencil

Erandi's Braids–Acrylics

Fin M'Coul–Rotring Artist Colors and pencil

Flicks–Two-color preseparated art

Francis, the Poor Man of Assisi–Transparent colored inks

The Friendly Beasts–Colored inks and pencil

Helga's Dowry–Transparent colored inks

The Hunter and the Animals–Transparent colored inks and tempera

Jamie O'Rourke and the Big Potato–Rotring Artist Colors

Jingle, the Christmas Clown–Acrylics

The Knight and the Dragon–Rotring Artist Colors

The Lady of Guadalupe–Watercolors, colored inks, and pencil

The Legend of the Bluebonnet–Rotring Artist Colors and tempera

The Legend of the Indian Paintbrush–Rotring Artist Colors and tempera

The Little Friar Who Flew–Three-color preseparated art

Marianna May and Nursey–Rotring Artist Colors

Mary Had a Little Lamb–Acrylics

Mary, the Mother of Jesus–Acrylics

Merry Christmas, Strega Nona–Rotring Artist Colors and transparent acrylics

Mice Squeak, We Speak–Acrylics

Miracle on 34th Street–Acrylics

The Mountains of Quilt–Rotring Artist Colors and colored pencils

My First Easter–Rotring Artist Colors

Nana Upstairs & Nana Downstairs–Three-color preseparated art

Nana Upstairs & Nana Downstairs, new edition–Transparent acrylics

Nicholas Bentley Stoningpot III–Rotring Artist Colors

The Night Before Christmas–Watercolors and colored inks

Now One Foot, Now the Other–Three-color preseparated art

Oliver Button Is a Sissy–Three-color preseparated art

Patrick, Patron Saint of Ireland–Acrylics

The Popcorn Book–Three-color preseparated art

The Quicksand Book–Three-color preseparated art

The Quilt Story–Acrylics

Sing, Pierrot, Sing–Rotring Artist Colors and tempera

Sound–Three-color preseparated art alternating with black and white

Strega Nona–Watercolors and pencil

Strega Nona, Her Story–Rotring Artist Colors and transparent acrylics

Strega Nona's Magic Lessons–Rotring Artist Colors and transparent acrylics

Strega Nona Meets Her Match–Rotring Artist Colors and transparent acrylics

The Tale of Rabbit and Coyote–Acrylics

Tom–Transparent acrylics

Tomie dePaola's Mother Goose–Transparent acrylics

Tomie dePaola's Book of Bible Stories–Transparent acrylics

Tomie dePaola's Book of Christmas Carols–Acrylics

Tomie dePaola's Favorite Nursery Tales–Transparent acrylics

Tomie's Little Mother Goose–Transparent acrylics

Tony's Bread–Transparent acrylics

The Triumphs of Fuzzy Fogtop–Watercolors and pencil

Wheels–Three-color preseparated art alternating with black and white

The Wonderful Dragon of Timlin–Three-color preseparated art

# Art and Photo Credits

Grateful acknowledgment is given here for the permissions to reprint images from Tomie dePaola's books to the following publishers and especially to Margaret Frith of G. P. Putnam's Sons, John Briggs of Holiday House, Louise Pelan of Harcourt Brace, and Rick Richter of Simon & Schuster for their help and generosity.

## DIAL BOOKS FOR YOUNG READERS

*The Triumphs of Fuzzy Fogtop* by Anne Rose. Illustrations copyright © 1979 by Tomie dePaola.

## HARCOURT BRACE

*Big Anthony and the Magic Ring.* Copyright © 1979 by Tomie dePaola.

*The Clown of God.* Copyright © 1978 by Tomie dePaola.

*Flicks.* Copyright © 1979 by Tomie dePaola.

*Helga's Dowry: A Troll Love Story.* Copyright © 1977 by Tomie dePaola.

*Merry Christmas, Strega Nona.* Copyright © 1986 by Tomie dePaola.

*Miracle on 34th Street* by Valentine Davies. Illustrations copyright © 1984 by Tomie dePaola.

*The Mountains of Quilt* by Nancy Willard. Illustrations copyright © 1987 by Tomie dePaola.

*Oliver Button Is a Sissy.* Copyright © 1979 by Tomie dePaola.

*Sing, Pierrot, Sing.* Copyright © 1983 by Tomie dePaola.

*Strega Nona's Magic Lessons.* Copyright © 1982 by Tomie dePaola.

## HOLIDAY HOUSE

*Christopher, the Holy Giant.* Copyright © 1994 by Tomie dePaola.

*The Cloud Book.* Copyright © 1975 by Tomie dePaola.

*An Early American Christmas.* Copyright © 1987 by Tomie dePaola.

*Fin M'Coul, the Giant of Knockmany Hill.* Copyright © 1981 by Tomie dePaola.

*Francis, the Poor Man of Assisi.* Copyright © 1982 by Tomie dePaola.

*The Hunter and the Animals.* Copyright © 1981 by Tomie dePaola.

*The Lady of Guadalupe.* Copyright © 1980 by Tomie dePaola.

*Marianna May and Nursey.* Copyright © 1983 by Tomie dePaola.

*Mary Had a Little Lamb* by Sarah Josepha Hale. Illustrations copyright © 1984 by Tomie dePaola.

*Mary, the Mother of Jesus.* Copyright © 1995 by Tomie dePaola.

*Nicholas Bentley Stoningpot III* by Ann McGovern. Illustrations copyright © 1982 by Tomie dePaola.

*The Night Before Christmas* by Clement C. Moore. Illustrations copyright © 1980 by Tomie dePaola.

*Patrick, Patron Saint of Ireland.* Copyright © 1992 by Tomie dePaola.

*The Popcorn Book.* Copyright © 1978 by Tomie dePaola.

*The Quicksand Book.* Copyright © 1977 by Tomie dePaola.

## G. P. PUTNAM'S SONS

*Alice Nizzy Nazzy* by Tony Johnston. Illustrations copyright © 1995 by Tomie dePaola.

*The Art Lesson.* Copyright © 1989 by Tomie dePaola.

*The Baby Sister.* Copyright © 1996 by Tomie dePaola.

*Big Anthony, His Story.* Copyright © 1998 by Tomie dePaola.

*Bill and Pete.* Copyright © 1978 by Tomie dePaola.

*Bill and Pete to the Rescue.* Copyright © 1998 by Tomie dePaola.

*Bonjour, Mr. Satie.* Copyright © 1991 by Tomie dePaola.

*Country Angel Christmas.* Copyright © 1995 by Tomie dePaola.

## UNCAPTIONED ILLUSTRATIONS

On the Wing of a Whitebird: A Tomie dePaola Resource Book, page 7

Country Angel Christmas, page 20

The Baby Sister, page 25

26 Fairmount Avenue, page 47

My First Easter, page 49

Francis, the Poor Man of Assisi, page 58

Miracle on 34th Street, page 65

The Night Before Christmas, page 69

Jingle, the Christmas Clown, page 75

The Legend of the Bluebonnet, page 77

Days of the Blackbird, page 80

The Legend of the Indian Paintbrush, page 83

Alice Nizzy Nazzy, LEFT; Strega Nona, Her Story, RIGHT, page 89

DePaola doodle, page 91

Mary Had a Little Lamb, page 101

Bonjour, Mr. Satie, pages 102, 211

The Knight and the Dragon, page 115

Sound, page 117

The Cloud Book, page 120

The Popcorn Book, page 125

Tomie dePaola's Mother Goose, pages 127, 128, 130

Francis, the Poor Man of Assisi, page 135

The Wonderful Dragon of Timlin, pages 145, 146

Jamie O'Rourke and the Big Potato, page 151

Big Anthony, His Story, page 153

Strega Nona doll, page 161

# Acknowledgements

I would like to thank Margaret Frith for her support and belief in my abilities to write this book, Patricia Lee Gauch for her encouragement, Karen Hanley and Carolyn Wiseman for their readings of early drafts of the manuscript, Karen Hoyle for generously opening the Kerlan Collection on a Saturday, Chere Elliott for her wordsmith counseling, Cecilia Yung and Donna Mark for their creative input, Bob Hechtel, special thanks for his invaluable research and careful attention to every detail, Tomie dePaola for being such a grand host, Trina Schart Hyman for her insightful Preface, Roger Crossgrove for his tales of Pratt days, Bear for patiently keeping me company during the writing process, and especially Don Elleman for being there through my computer glitches and other first-time author traumas.

# Index

An asterisk indicates a book written and/or illustrated by Tomie dePaola; page numbers in italics indicate photographs or illustrations.